a Jim Pattison Company

EXECUTIVE VICE PRESIDENT, INTELLECTUAL PROPERTY Norm Deska

SENIOR DIRECTOR, PUBLISHING & LICENSING Amanda Joiner

EDITORIAL MANAGER Carrie Bolin

EDITOR Jessica Firpi

PROOFREADER Rachel Paul

DESIGNER Rose Audette

CONTRIBUTORS Luis Fuentes, Jordie R. Orlando

REPROGRAPHICS *POST LLC

COVER DESIGN Rose Audette

IN APPRECIATION
VICE PRESIDENT, EXHIBITS AND ARCHIVES, 1978-2018 Edward Meyer

VERY SPECIAL THANKS TO
Maureen Chant
Robert Goforth
John Graziano
Colton Kruse
Marcie Pikel
Sabrina Sieck

ISBN: 978-1-60991-240-6

For more information regarding permission, contact:
VP Intellectual Property
Ripley Entertainment Inc.
7576 Kingspointe Parkway, Suite 188
Orlando, Florida 32819
Email: publishing@ripleys.com
www.ripleys.com/books

Manufactured in China in June 2018 by Leo Paper
First Printing

Library of Congress Control Number: 2018947700

PUBLISHER'S NOTE
While every effort has been made to verify the accuracy of the entries in this book, the Publisher cannot be held responsible for any errors contained in the work. They would be glad to receive any information from readers.

WARNING
Some of the stunts and activities are undertaken by experts and should not be attempted by anyone without adequate training and supervision.

"Truth is stranger than fiction."
—Robert Ripley

CONTENTS

Letter from
Jim Pattison

"There are not many companies that can survive 100 years in any business and stay relevant. Ripley's has been able to do that."

—Jim Pattison, Chairman & CEO of The Jim Pattison Group

Believe it or not. Robert Ripley coined the phrase that has become a household expression to this day, 100 years later. You still hear people saying it all the time. I think it's remarkable that any company continues on for 100 years, but Ripley's is a brand that's a little more unique and a lot more special.

When we bought Ripley's in 1985, I'd heard of the company, of course, but I didn't know much about it. I was in the office building of the World's Fair in Vancouver when I got a phone call from a Ripley's Believe It or Not! licensee who told me that he thought the company could use a fresh start and that I should buy it.

At the time, the closest I'd been to being involved in an entertainment company was what I was currently doing—putting on Expo 86 in Vancouver. The event had 22 million people, and there was certainly a lot of entertainment there. The idea was intriguing, and after researching the opportunity further, we decided to bring Ripley's on as The Pattison Group's newest acquisition.

It was true what the licensee had said—the company definitely needed improvements. The first thing we did was decide who was going to run it. It wasn't long before we gave the opportunity to Bob Masterson, who had worked with Ripley's in San Francisco and many other locations. The new management team really took over the company and started to do something positive with it.

Ripley's is a fun company—and we're in the business of selling fun. The Ripley's team realized that there's a lot more you can do when you're in the family entertainment business, not just the museum business—the sky's the limit. It was this realization that really helped grow the company from the initial eight museums we had when we acquired it into the world-class attractions company it is today.

As the company grew, acquiring new attractions like 3D Motion Theaters, the team was thinking even bigger. Bob's idea was to build an aquarium, though not just any aquarium. He wanted to change the face of the aquarium business and instead of them being educational institutions to make them into entertaining, family-friendly destinations that people would love to spend time in and revisit again and again.

At first, I didn't think this was a viable idea. I wondered why would we want to get into a business that we didn't know anything about, especially one where you had to worry about keeping your attraction (the fish) alive? We took it to the board of directors, and they decided to support it.

We started with an aquarium business in Myrtle Beach, South Carolina, but not everything went according to plan. The costs were way over budget—double what we initially thought. But Ripley's built a wonderful aquarium, and the revenues generated by it made up for the budget concerns, so much so that we opened a second aquarium in Gatlinburg, Tennessee.

By the time Bob retired in 2009, Ripley's had grown significantly and gained the momentum it needed to continue growing. Bob passed the presidential torch to Jim Pattison Jr. when he retired, and under Jim's leadership, we have since opened a third more successful aquarium in Toronto, Canada, as well as many other attractions.

JIMMY at Ripley's Aquarium of Canada.

From its modest start in 1985, the company now has more than 100 attractions around the world. We're going for 200, and with the current management team in place, I believe we'll get there.

Ripley's has given us a lot of great experiences over the years, and a lot of odd ones, too. One piece of advice—don't try taking a shrunken head through customs. It might liven up the talk you're preparing to give, but it will tie you up for hours while you're trying to explain to the customs agents why you have it. Trust me on this.

There are not many companies that can survive 100 years in any business and stay relevant. Ripley's has been able to do that, and that's a great credit to the brand and the management for keeping it relatable and interesting over the years. People are fascinated by the bizarre, the strange, the unusual, and Ripley's owns that space in the attractions industry.

Ripley's came to us as an opportunity, and what an opportunity it's been. This company has changed a lot in its 100-year history, and certainly in the last 34 years that we have owned it. No company can be successful without skillful management, which is what gives me such confidence in the future of Ripley's. I believe this company has a terrific future ahead. In my opinion, it's just getting started.

Above, **JIMMY** and Jim Jr. with the Ripley Entertainment management team posing with the Marilyn dress at Partners in Pride 2017.

Introduction by
Jim Davis

"The care that Robert Ripley gave to the drawings, as well as the entertainment factor and the professionalism with which he'd done every panel, absolutely set a standard for the kind of cartoonist I wanted to be."

—Jim Davis, creator of the *Garfield* comic strip

There's nothing like Ripley's. Name something that's just like Ripley's. There really isn't anything. For 100 years, this unique company has stirred the imaginations of millions of people around the globe, inciting awe, amazement, and genuine disbelief. I've been along for the ride for 65 of those 100 years, first as an avid fan and later as a fellow cartoonist and then as a friend of this great company's leaders.

As a kid growing up on a farm near Fairmount, Indiana, the weekly Sunday cartoon from *Ripley's Believe It or Not!* in the *Marion Chronicle Tribune* was my window into a world much larger than I knew then. I looked forward to that Sunday paper—the cartoon wasn't just informative; it was fun. It was shocking. And I loved every bit of it.

It made me wonder about the people Ripley featured: how did they DO that? Why would they do that? I devoured the stories about objects and artifacts, lost in the depths of faraway locations and all the excitement and mystery that swirled around them. It just fired my imagination to read about these things, to see them.

It also made me wonder how he did it. The cartoon was done in such a beautiful illustration style. There was no right-hand or left-hand lean to his drawing. Everything was in perfect proportion and so detailed. The illustrations were amazing in and of themselves.

It was that detail and artistry that inspired the approach that I take to creating my own work. The care that Robert Ripley gave to the drawings, as well as the entertainment factor and the professionalism with which he'd done every panel absolutely set a standard for the kind of cartoonist I wanted to be.

So, it wasn't a surprise to me years down the road in my own career when a certain fat cat of mine decided to pay homage to the company that I drew inspiration from with a little series of his own called *Garfield's Believe It or Don't!*.

This company is an icon that continues to inspire, astonish, and delight people around the world, bringing families and friends together to share in everything odd and amazing. There truly has been nothing like Ripley's Believe It or Not! in the past 100 years, and as this one-and-only company embarks on its next 100, you can believe there will never be another one like it.

The Man

Foreword by Neal Thompson

As a biographer, I seek inspiration from the lives of the people I write about. I love learning about forgotten or misunderstood characters in history, or learning more about someone I thought I knew. That was certainly the case with Ripley, and what I admired about him was that his success was based on his devotion to people like himself—odd people, misfits, people who came from dark places.

As a writer, I'm fascinated by underdogs, and at its core, Ripley's life was that of an underdog.

He was a man who overcame challenges and lived a big life, a great life. But how did he do it? How did this kid—a fatherless loner, a dirt-poor outsider, a funny-looking bucktoothed stutterer—become a millionaire playboy, friend of Hollywood actresses and U.S. presidents, sports stars, and royalty? My search for answers drove me to spend five years researching his life and writing his biography, *A Curious Man*.

Though Ripley considered himself a rube and a farm boy, he indulged in a lifestyle as risky as any of the extreme characters in his cartoons. He taught Americans to gape with respect at the weirdness of man and nature. I was awed and charmed by his eagerness, his adventurousness. He appreciated the extremes of life—sports, endurance, religion, the extremes of the material world, of science, and of nature. He was extreme and intrepid in everything he did, from his global travels to his on-location radio broadcasts to his relationships, his clothes, his homes.

His timing was impeccable; he tapped into something America needed—entertainment and escape—during dark and difficult times. He did it by championing the little guy or girl, the person with grit and determination. He spoke to the Walter Mittys of the world and taught them, by example and through his cartoon, that their fantasies could come true. He challenged them, and he taught me—taught us all—to believe in the unbelievable.

It's amazing that the phrase Ripley coined remains part of the English lexicon a century later, but the spirit of Ripley lives on, too, as do the aspirations that Ripley embodied: voyeurism, exhibitionism, the appreciation of freakishness, oddities, pranks of nature, and the extreme capabilities of human beings and the human spirit. He was mostly hopeful, and until his later years, was constantly inspired by the world.

"The more I see of the world the more I like it," he wrote while traveling through South America in 1925. "It's a pretty good little old place after all, and I have little time for the gloomers who are eternally shrieking that this old mud ball is rolling to the bow wows." I'm not sure what he'd think of our world today. (Although I'd like to think he'd be great on Twitter.) Still, I try to remind myself of Ripley's advice to "carry along with you a lively imagination and plenty of romance in your soul."

As he put it, "Some of the most wonderful things in the world will seem dull and drab unless you view them in the proper light."

Ripley taught me to seek the proper light, and I'm grateful that I got to know the man.

"Ripley taught me to seek the proper light, and I'm grateful that I got to know the man."

—Neal Thompson, journalist and the author of five books, including *A Curious Man*, the official Robert Ripley biography

NEAL with political commentator and TV host John Oliver.

"His timing was impeccable; he tapped into something America needed—entertainment and escape—during dark and difficult times."

—Neal Thompson

NEAL giving a talk on Robert Ripley at the University of Mary Washington.

Above, **A CURIOUS MAN,** the official Robert Ripley biography.

It's hard to describe a man who was indescribable, but Robert Ripley was just that. Equal parts explorer, reporter, artist, and collector, he was a seeker. Just what did he seek out? *The unusual.*

"Anybody who is born in Santa Rosa must turn out to be either an artist or a poet, for the spirit of the hills gets into your blood out there."
—Robert Ripley

Who Was Mr. Robert Ripley?

His strange and brilliant life began on February 22, 1890, although he would later claim to be born on Christmas Day, Christmas Eve, and varying birth years. His mother, Lillie Belle, was already pregnant when she married his father, Isaac David Ripley.

RIPLEY aged 5 months.

Wm. Shaw, Third St. Gallery, SAN

LeRoy Robert Ripley—Roy to his parents—was energetic but shy, mocked in school because of his protruding buck teeth. To top it off, he also had a stutter, which made reciting poems and essays in class traumatic. His only solace came in the form of drawing pictures, scribbling, and constantly sketching.

RIPLEY'S childhood home.

With two busy working parents, Ripley was left to his own devices as a child, free to read eccentric newspaper stories (yellow journalism), explore the exotic restaurants and shops of Chinatown, and visit the wondrous Ringling Brothers Circus when it came to town.

Humble Beginnings

By the time Ripley entered high school in 1904, he'd grown athletic and joined the baseball team—although he never lost his awkwardness or, most importantly, his artistic passion.

His family couldn't afford art supplies, but even that could not stop Ripley. Instead of drawing paper, Ripley used butcher paper, scrap paper, notebooks, and textbooks. In place of an easel, he used a cutting board.

"THE VILLAGE BELL WAS SLOWLY RINGING"

When his father died suddenly in September 1905, Ripley was left alone with his mother and two siblings, Ethel and 16-month-old Douglas. Despite his mother urging him to get a "real job," Ripley continued to draw, even earning some money drawing posters and advertisements for the local baseball team (while doing an assortment of odd jobs, of course).

Lured by the stories of staff artists at San Francisco papers making $1,000 a year or more, he mailed off a one-panel cartoon to *LIFE* magazine in New York. The 1907 sketch played with homonyms: showcasing a pretty woman wringing out wet clothes, the caption read, "The Village Bell Was Slowly Ringing."

Although he'd already dropped out, Ripley drew his high school commencement program cover, signing the drawing "By LeRoy Ripley." Five days later, *LIFE* published the "Village Bell" cartoon, which ran in the June 18 issue. The $8 he received as payment emboldened him to make his career in cartooning.

Early Work

Ripley's first cartoonist job at the *San Francisco Bulletin* would take him away from Santa Rosa for good. He moved to the big city, a small fish—with no formal art training—in a slightly bigger pond.

He soon found himself overshadowed by his more experienced colleagues. He was fired after only four months on the job.

Ripley rebounded by snagging a job with a competing newspaper—the *San Francisco Chronicle*. He signed up for art classes five mornings a week and then labored late into the evenings drawing hundreds of cartoons. His efforts paid off. Less than a year into the job, he was assigned as the sports cartoonist for the big boxing fight between Jim Jeffries and Jack Johnson.

But it all came crashing down once again—demanding $25 a week from his boss resulted in Ripley accidentally quitting the *Chronicle*.

This page, **RIPLEY** with his fellow cartoonists at the *San Francisco Chronicle.*

ROBERT RIPLEY

When asked whom he studied under, Ripley would say "I studied under the stars in Santa Rosa."

THE LIGHT THAT NEVER FAILS.—By Ripley.

The Big Apple

I t wasn't until Ripley moved to New York in 1912 and later started working at the *New York Globe* that the wheels were set in motion for the career of a lifetime.

THE FATAL TEN.—*By Ripley.*

MIKE GIBBONS'S BIG BROTHER.—

BESIDES, THOM IS AGGRESSIVE

NOW RUB YOUR NOSE LIKE THIS

RIPLEY COPYRIGHT 1918.

TOM GIBBONS — AS GOOD AS HIS BROTHER

'COURSE MIKE TAUGHT HIM HOW

RIPLEY

He started out depicting sporting events (especially his favorite, baseball), and thanks to a newly formed newspaper syndicate, his toons were seen by hundreds of thousands of readers across the United States—even appearing in, ironically, the *San Francisco Bulletin*.

Not long after he debuted at the *Globe*, his editors made him change his name. They couldn't have a "LeRoy" in the sports department. Thus, he became Robert Ripley and, later, Robert L. Ripley.

In 1913, the *Globe* sent the newly minted Robert Ripley on a trip to Europe—a lavish and rare opportunity for a rookie staffer. The *Globe* announced the grand trip with a huge headline atop the sports page reading "RIPLEY IS OFF FOR EUROPE TODAY," along with a six-column cartoon featuring a Ripley self-portrait.

Despite his surroundings, Ripley kept his drawings strictly sports-related and only deviated from the itinerary once, resulting in an exasperated conversation in broken English with a taxi driver in Paris. (Ripley only spoke English.) The *Globe* heralded his return with another six-column caricature.

Then war broke out. With sporting events mostly on hold during World War I, Ripley drew patriotic cartoons, and some of his wartime sketches were used as recruitment posters.

Champs & Chumps

Believe it or not, the cartoon that started it all was not called "Believe It or Not!"

When World War I ended and Ripley resumed regularly drawing sports cartoons, a slow news day made him return to an old concept that he'd experimented with back in the winter of 1916.

The "Champs and Chumps" cartoon appeared in the *New York Globe* on December 19, 1918. Featuring nine unbelievable athletic feats culled from Ripley's personal collection of daring sports, extreme activities, and far-off places, the second cartoon with similar content didn't appear until 10 months later—the first with the exact title "Believe It or Not."

The eventual series launched the catchphrase that became a household saying, as well as the entity that would become the Ripley brand.

Ripley displayed the toon that started it all in his extravagant BION Island mansion. He hung the panel behind a backlit mirror above the massive, ornate fireplace and then would flip a light switch to illuminate the hidden cartoon.

"The first 'Believe It or Not' cartoon was an accident. I had been drawing cartoons for the sports pages for some time when, in the course of a day's work, I hurriedly put together a few athletic oddities that happened to be lying on my desk and made them up into a cartoon—never for a moment expecting that it meant any more than a day's work done. . . and for the want of a better caption I called it 'Believe It or Not.'"

—Robert Ripley

This page, RIPLEY holds the "Champs and Chumps" panel, regarded as the first *Believe It or Not* cartoon.

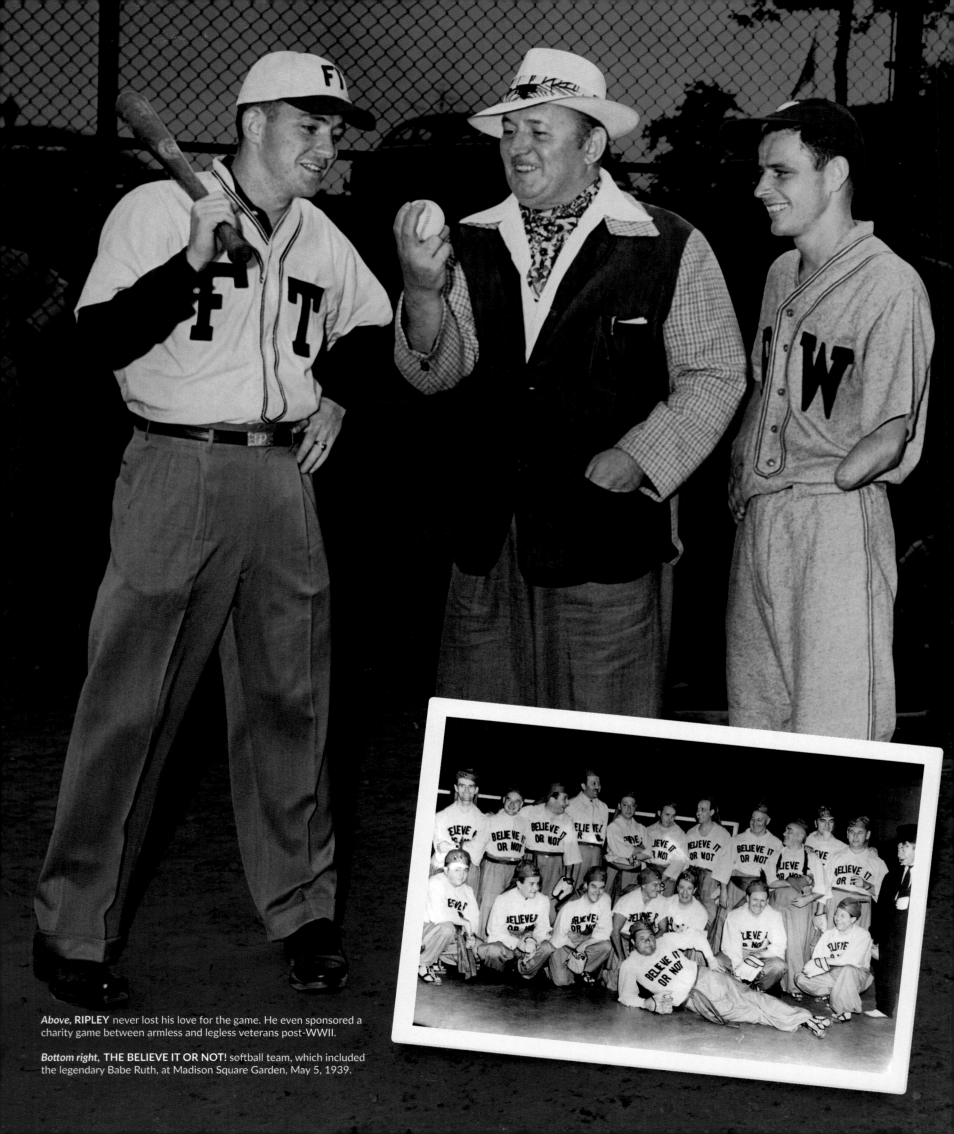

Above, **RIPLEY** never lost his love for the game. He even sponsored a charity game between armless and legless veterans post-WWII.

Bottom right, **THE BELIEVE IT OR NOT!** softball team, which included the legendary Babe Ruth, at Madison Square Garden, May 5, 1939.

On the Ball

Ripley spent as much time devoted to his cartoons as he did playing baseball and dreaming of one day joining his favorite team, the New York Giants. His dream almost came true.

In early 1913, Ripley was sent on the road with the New York Giants to cover their spring training in Marlin, Texas. With his formative years spent playing for local semi-professional teams, Ripley attracted the coaches' attention, and they invited him to workout with the team.

In a cruel twist of fate, Ripley was called in to pitch—and fractured his arm. Other stories claim Ripley signed a minor-league contract with the Giants before he broke his arm, but either way, the injury cemented his career path.

Claude SANBORN Boots SCARLETT Harold LOUGHERY Believe It or Not! RIPLEY Joe SCHMIDT Walter COFFEY Harry McNAMARA Earl WEIR Jack TOWEY

SANTA ROSA BASEBALL TEAM 1909

Above, **RIPLEY** with his semi-professional Santa Rosa city baseball team.

"It ruined me as a baseball player. And it made me a cartoonist."
—Robert Ripley

Handball

Focused on staying fit and healthy, Ripley joined and moved into the New York Athletic Club (NYAC) in 1918 and then promptly became obsessed with handball.

No. 114R

Price 25 Cents

SPALDING'S
ATHLETIC LIBRARY

HAND BALL GUIDE

AMERICAN SPO...
45 R...

ROBERT L. RIPLEY.
The famous cartoonist, whose skill at handball is only exceeded by his love of the game.

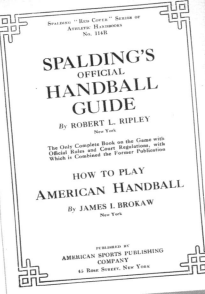

Spalding "Red Cover" Series of Athletic Handbooks
No. 114R

SPALDING'S
OFFICIAL
HANDBALL GUIDE

By ROBERT L. RIPLEY
New York

The Only Complete Book on the Game with Official Rules and Court Regulations, with Which is Combined the Former Publication

HOW TO PLAY
AMERICAN HANDBALL

By JAMES I. BROKAW
New York

PUBLISHED BY
AMERICAN SPORTS PUBLISHING COMPANY
45 Rose Street, New York

Left, **PUBLISHED** in late 1923, the *Spalding's Official Handball Guide* was written by Ripley while in between newspaper jobs. Six years later, another Ripley book would grab the world's attention.

Above, **RIPLEY** played in citywide and national championship tournaments regularly during the 1920s.

"It is the most natural thing in the world to slap a ball with the hand."
—Robert Ripley

Left, **RIPLEY** became the 1925 New York Athletic Club (NYAC) singles handball champion. Here he is being presented a trophy for handball circa 1926.

Ripley's Ramble

In December 1922, Ripley embarked on a four-month-long adventure that would take him around the world for the first time. He would eventually become a member of the exclusive Circumnavigators Club.

"All my life I have waited for this day... To go 'round the world is a youthful dream—a dream that gradually fades away with the years... Such an opportunity comes seldom, if ever, in a lifetime... And while on the way I will tell you about it... I hope to interest you."

—Robert Ripley

This page, **RIPLEY** in front of the Taj Mahal in Agra, India.

RIPLEY in Jerusalem, Israel.

RIPLEY in Guangzhou (then Canton), China.

RIPLEY inside the Colosseum in Rome, Italy.

RIPLEY in front of the Pareshnath Jain Temple in Calcutta, India.

Traveling by train, steamship, army transport, rickshaw, sedan chair, elephant, horse, camel, and on foot, Ripley made his own itinerary, and each dispatch and sketch detailed the wonders of the unknown.

Soon his travelogue began to take shape—a true blogger, so to speak— and he teased his audience with playful truths. One day he wrote that he "slept with a Dutch wife" in Java but then the next day confessed that a Dutch wife was really an oblong pillow.

His journey took him through China, the country that eventually became his favorite, and all the while, he always wore a suit and bow tie, sketch pad in hand.

RIPLEY aboard the SS Laconia.

Life and Love

On October 23, 1919, Ripley ended his bachelor days and married 18-year-old Beatrice Roberts, a teen beauty queen from Boston who moved to the Big Apple to become a dancer.

They had their first date the night he drew his famous "Champs and Chumps" cartoon in 1918. She called him Roy, and he called her Bea.

The honeymoon period quickly dissipated. The pair separated after just three months and then divorced a few years later.

RIPLEY and his first wife, Beatrice Roberts, on the beach.

Ruth Ross was the mysterious woman who became Ripley's lover and constant travel companion, even on payroll as a Believe It or Not Inc. employee.

She took the reins organizing his vast BION Island home—hiring all the domestic help and arranging his antique furniture and artwork—before he moved in permanently.

It was somewhat of a hush-hush affair because Oakie (as he called her) was married to someone else.

RUTH ROSS spoke English with an accent, pronouncing "OK" like "oakie," so Ripley nicknamed her Oakie.

This page, Top right, **RIPLEY** with Ruth Ross in Hawaii.

"The world is round, but a little bumpy."
—Robert Ripley

EARL CARROLL BEAUTIES enjoying a relaxing treatment in the Howard Cabinet, which was a waterproof heat box used like a steam sauna.

Print & Spectacle

I n 1929, Ripley published the very first *Believe It or Not!* book, which flew off bookstore shelves.

The 188-page book received rave reviews. Walter Winchell, well-known newspaper and radio gossip commentator, devoted a full column to it in the *Evening Graphic*. Over the next 20 years, Ripley's book would sell more than 2.2 million copies, going into its 40th printing.

Right, **RIPLEY** holds a giant version of his first book with the dust jacket showing the well-known "Marching Chinese" cartoon from April 1928.

Below, **RIPLEY** at a book signing for the second *Believe It or Not!* book published in 1931.

Success & Progress

The very first *Believe It or Not!* book's fame triggered the first Ripley museum at the 1933 World's Fair in Chicago.

The museum, an "Odditorium," saw an astounding two million visitors. Inside the museum were dozens of Ripley's famous cartoons, live performers, and hundreds of strange and exotic artifacts Ripley acquired from his worldly travels. There were human bone outfits from Tibet, medieval chastity belts, and of course, a pair of shrunken heads from the Jivaro tribe of Ecuador. In fact, Ripley traveled so much that by this time he already had a catchy nickname—"The Modern Marco Polo."

The success of the first Odditorium led to several more appearances at world expositions across the country.

Below, NEWSPAPER *cutout for the 1933 Chicago show.*

"BELIEVE IT OR NOT"—This Ripley "Odditorium" exhibit at A Century of Progress draws thousands daily to see the oddities, who appear in person on sixteen different stages. It is one of the most popular sights at the fair.—Herald and Examiner photo.

This page, **THE RIPLEY** Odditorium at the 1934 encore show at the World's Fair in Chicago.

Right, **ADVERTISEMENT** for the Chicago 1933 World's Fair Odditorium.

Below, **SOUVENIR STAMP** for the 1934 Chicago show.

At Chicago Exhibit of Believe-It-Or-Nots

Thousands of Americans who have followed the famous Believe-It-Or-Not Cartoons of Robert Ripley are seeing the actual Believe-It-Or-Nots housed in the palatial Ripley "Odditorium" at the Chicago Century of Progress. Included among the exhibits are (left) Singhlee, a Hindu who can grasp a red-hot metal bar and put it to his mouth; (below left) Albert Nelson and his one-man mechanical band of thirty instruments; and (below right) Blystone, the rice writer.

RIPLEY BELIEVE IT OR NOT

CENTURY OF PROGRESS

CHICAGO AMERICAN — SOUVENIR STAMP

F. L. BLYSTONE of ARDARA, Pa. WROTE 2871 LEGIBLE LETTERS ON A SINGLE GRAIN OF RICE! NATIONAL PRIZE WINNER Believe It or Not Contest

The Most Popular Man in America

Ripley was trending on all platforms. In 1929 alone, he received a million letters, nearly 3,000 a day.

In a 1936 poll, Ripley was voted the most popular American, beating out President Roosevelt, champion boxer Jack Dempsey, and Hollywood actor James Cagney.

This page, **RIPLEY** signing autographs.

President? Youths Prefer Believe It or Not's Job

NEW YORK (AP)—President of the United States—this proverbial ambition of almost every mother in the nation for her son—has met a rebuff. Eleven thousand youngsters between eight and 17, making up the Boy's Club of New York, today are on record as relegating the chief executive's job to a place far down in the list of popular aims.

The group, on the crowded East Side, representing almost every conceivable race and creed, was polled on the question: "If you had your choice of all the jobs in the world whose job would you want?"

Robert ("Believe It or Not") Ripley got the most votes with J. Edgar Hoover, chief of the bureau of investigation of the United States department of justice, second, and James Cagney, motion picture star, third. The President stood seventh on the list, just below Dizzy Dean, of the baseball diamond, Police Commissioner Lewis J. Valentine of New York and Jack D

ROBERT L. RIPLEY

RIPLEY MOST POPULAR
Boys Rank President's Job Low

NEW YORK, April 5. — (AP) — The ambition to be President of the United States was disclosed to-day as far from the most popular aim of 11,000 youngsters between eight and eighteen years of age making up the Boys' Club of New York.

The group, on the crowded East Side, representing almost every conceivable race and creed, was polled on the question: "If you had your choice of all the jobs in the world, whose job would you

Robert ("Believe It or Not") Rip-ley got the most votes, with J. Edgar Hoover, chief of the bureau of investigation of the United States department of justice second and James Cagney, motion picture star, third. The President stood seventh on the list, just below Dizzy Dean, of the baseball diamond, Police Commissioner Lewis J. Valentine of New York and Jack Dempsey, former heavyweight champion of the world.

King Edward VIII of England stood eighth on the list and Mayor F. H. LaGuardia ninth.

Boys Would Rather Be Ripley Than President, Who's 7th In Poll

New York, April 5 (AP)—The ambition to be president of the United States was disclosed to-day as far from the most popular aim of the 11,000 youngsters, be-tween 8 and 18, who make up the boys' club of New York.

The East Side group, represent-ing almost every conceivable race and creed, w

didn't want to be President be-cause the Chief Executive "was only sure of his job for four years." He added he'd rather be chief judge, with a life-time job.

Another regarded the Presi-dent's job as "too tough—you have to please everybody."

King Edward of E

RIPLEY LEADS AS BOYS' IDOL
G-Man Hoover Ranks Second, Roosevelt Seventh

Cagney Third In Vote Cast by 11,000 New York Youths

NEW YORK, April 4 (U.S.). New York boys between eight and 18 would rather step into the shoes of Robert "Believe It Or Not" Ripley

Ripley   Hoover

the first 10 "winners" in the order of popularity:
1, Robert Ripley; 2, J. Edgar

Winchell 10th (Haw!) But Bernie Isn't Even Mentioned

Hoover; 3, James Cagney; 4, Dizzy Dean; 5, Police Commissioner Lewis J. Valentine; 6, Jack Demp-sey; 7, President Franklin D. Roosevelt; 8, King Edward VIII of England; 9, Mayor Fiorello La Guardia, and 10, Walter Winchell.

Mussolini failed to make the first 10, while Major Bowes got the gong himself by showing up in the "also rans." Vice President John Garner was awarded one vote. In this class also were Ad-miral Byrd, Bobby Jones, Freddie Bartholomew and Col. Lindbergh.

Ripley, Hoover And Cagney Top Poll As Boys' Club Idols; Roosevelt Seventh

By The United Press

NEW YORK, April 5.—Robert Ripley, J. Edgar Hoover and James Cagney, cartoonist, chief G-man and movie he-man, ran off with the honors tonight in a "hero wor-ship" poll at the Boys' club of New York, whose 11,000 East Side mem-bers include every race and creed in the city.

President Roosevelt was placed seventh in the balloting by the youths, ranging in age from 8 to 18. They were asked in a question-naire:

"If you had your choices of all the jobs in the world, whose job would you want?"

These were their first 10 choices, in the order of popularity:
1. Robert Ripley.
2. J. Edgar Hoover.
3. James Cagney.
4. Dizzy Dean.
5. Lewis J. Valentine, New York police commissioner.
6. Jack Dempsey.
7. President Franklin D. Roose-velt.
8. King Edward VIII of England.
9. Mayor Fiorello H. LaGuardia.
10. Walter Winchell.

be President because the nation's chief executive was "only sure of his job for four years," and added, "I'd rather be chief judge (justice) he gets his job for life."

Some of the boys wanted to be King Edward VIII, of England, be-cause "he's not married."

Mussolini failed to make the first 10, but showed up in eleventh place. Major Edward Bowes, radio's ama-teur impresario, got the gong him-self by applying for a job from Vice-President John N. Garner was awarded one vote.

In explaining the reasons for the selections, one youth sagely charac-terized President Roosevelt's job as being "too tough, you have to please

Ripley was chosen by many be-cause he is "one of the most interest-ing people and maker" and "he gets around a lot."

They thought Mayor LaGuardia had a good position as "mayor of the greatest city in the world;" also, one reply stated, "he takes the rap when there's snow on the streets."

The also-rans included Admiral Richard E. Byrd, Bobby Jones, Bill Tilden, Freddie Bartholomew, Cap-tain Eddie V. Rickenbacker and Colonel Charles A. Lindbergh.

"Thereafter I made a 'Believe It or Not' cartoon a week. A year later, I made two a week, and soon the demand came that I make one every day. Now it looks as though I will never do anything else. And I don't care if I do."
—Robert Ripley

Ripley soon started receiving some very strange mail—a single stamp with the address and a 47-word message on the back, or envelopes addressed to "the damndest liar in the world."

Things got so out of hand that in April 1930, the U.S. postmaster general tried to curb the amount of work postal workers were putting into sorting Ripley's fan mail. "Postal clerks have had to devote too much time recently to deciphering freak letters intended for Ripley," he said.

The REMARKABLE ROBERT RIPLEY LETTER
POSTMARKED IN THE TOWNS OF "ROBERT" AND "RIPLEY".
"RIPLEY" CANCELLED ON RIPLEY'S BIRTHDAY-XMAS DAY
"ROBERT" CANCELLED ON NEW YEAR'S DAY.

THIS SIDE OF CARD IS FOR ADDRESS

Send it to Ripley

Life of the Party

R ipley earned a reputation for throwing extravagant parties.

In 1934, Ripley purchased BION Island in Mamaroneck, New York—a mansion on a private island where he could relax and party among all the foreign artifacts he had collected.

This page, **RIPLEY** later bought his Manhattan apartment, called Nirvana, which was decked out in Asian-themed décor, eventually owning four properties at the time of his death.

B. A. ROLFE

LI LING AI

DOUG RIPLEY

HAZEL STORER

DOUG STORER

BUGS BAER

Above, **RIPLEY** demonstrates his skill with chopsticks to friends Anna May Wong (left) and Ann Sheridan (right), circa 1940.

He'd invite almost everyone he knew—including friends, family, politicians, sports stars, visiting royalty, and celebrities—to his island for lavish dinners, costume parties, and barbecues thrown for any and every occasion.

BOXER Jack Dempsey horsing around with Ripley. Dempsey, the world heavyweight champion from 1919 to 1926, was a good friend of Ripley's.

WEARING his charity softball uniform, Ripley poses with comedians Olsen and Johnson.

RIPLEY rubbed elbows with the rich and famous, including child actress Shirley Temple in the mid-1930s.

RIPLEY receiving a sombrero from Portuguese singer and film star Carmen Miranda circa 1940.

The guest lists ranged from boxer Jack Dempsey and entertainer Carmen Miranda to World War I hero and race car driver Eddie Rickenbacker.

This page, **RIPLEY** with entertainers Carmen Miranda, Ole Olsen, Ray Bolger, Ella Logan, and Chic Johnson, singing at a New York City party around 1940.

Once bullied in school for his bad teeth, Ripley eventually became the most eligible bachelor in New York, and would often be seen around the city accompanied by a beautiful young actress, singer, or dancer—not to mention all his lady companions that visited BION Island.

The Man's Best Friends

When not surrounded by his adoring fans, famous friends, or women, Ripley preferred the company of his many pets.

THERE were spaniels and collies, and Ripley even raised Dalmatians and donated the pups to Mamaroneck, New York's fire department.

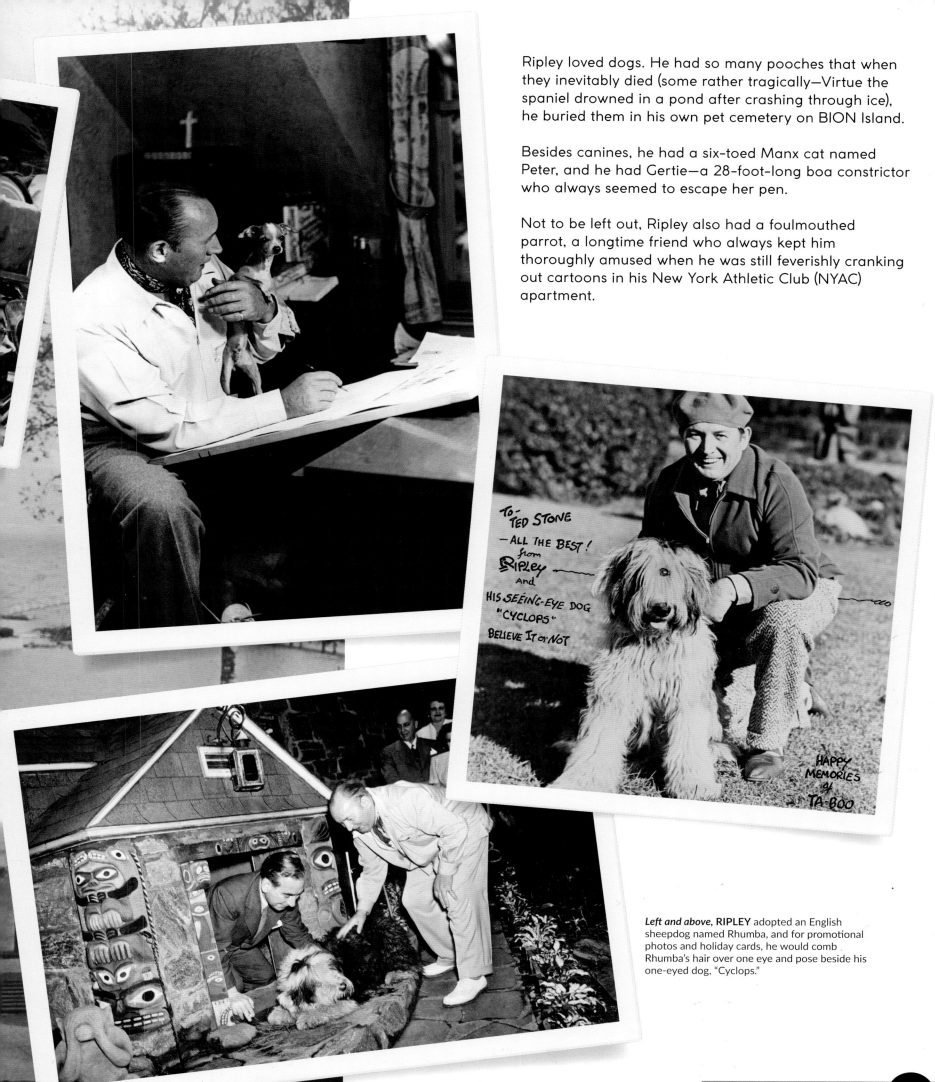

Ripley loved dogs. He had so many pooches that when they inevitably died (some rather tragically—Virtue the spaniel drowned in a pond after crashing through ice), he buried them in his own pet cemetery on BION Island.

Besides canines, he had a six-toed Manx cat named Peter, and he had Gertie—a 28-foot-long boa constrictor who always seemed to escape her pen.

Not to be left out, Ripley also had a foulmouthed parrot, a longtime friend who always kept him thoroughly amused when he was still feverishly cranking out cartoons in his New York Athletic Club (NYAC) apartment.

To TED STONE — ALL THE BEST! from RIPLEY and HIS SEEING-EYE DOG "CYCLOPS" BELIEVE IT or NOT

HAPPY MEMORIES of TA-BOO

Left and above, **RIPLEY** adopted an English sheepdog named Rhumba, and for promotional photos and holiday cards, he would comb Rhumba's hair over one eye and pose beside his one-eyed dog, "Cyclops."

Death of an Icon

Ripley died in May 1949. He had collapsed on the set of his weekly TV show during the 13th episode, while he was on stage discussing the military funeral hymn "Taps."

After the near disastrous live show, he admitted himself into a hospital for a checkup that revealed he had a heart condition, although not critical. On the night of his second day in the hospital, he had a fatal heart attack.

A funeral service was held at St. James Episcopal Church just six blocks away from Ripley's New York apartment. Hundreds attended the service, including celebrities, journalists, athletes, and cartoonists.

RIPLEY with the crown collection shown on the final show.

This page, **RIPLEY** was buried back in his hometown of Santa Rosa, California, in the Odd Fellows section of the city cemetery.

AMONG the honorary pallbearers were William Randolph Hearst's son, publisher Max Schuster, and former heavyweight champ Jack Dempsey.

The soul departed in the Lord does not die, it returneth to God, who is the Giver of life.

IN LOVING MEMORY OF

Robert L. Ripley

Died May 27, 1949

THE Lord is my shepherd, I shall not want. He maketh me to lie down in green pastures. He leadeth me beside the still waters. He restoreth my soul. He leadeth me in the paths of righteousness for His name's sake. Yea, though I walk through the valley of the shadow of death, I will fear no evil: for thou art with me, thy rod and thy staff they comfort me. Thou preparest a table before me in the presence of mine enemies. Thou anointest my head with oil: my cup runneth over. Surely goodness and mercy shall follow me all the days of my life: and I will dwell in the house of the Lord for ever. Amen.

"THE ABBEY"
Home for Funerals
132 E. 70th St.   New York
Tel. REgent 4-3500
James A. McCabe   PRINTED IN ITALY
97

Left, **THE FRONT** and back of the funeral card handed out at the service.

Below, **RIPLEY'S** longtime friend Arthur "Bugs" Baer wrote a piece for the *New York Journal-American* that appeared on Saturday, May 28, 1949.

Ripley Rites Are Attended By Notables

New York Journal-American

6—Sat., May 28, 1949

Bob Ripley's Death Is a Tough One to Believe, Says 'Bugs' Baer

("If Ripley told me I had two heads I would go out and buy two hats." Thus columnist Arthur (Bugs) Baer eulogizes his pal of nearly 40 years, Robert Ripley, originator of the "Believe It Or Not" cartoon. Baer spoke with Ripley by telephone minutes before the cartoonist died suddenly of a heart attack yesterday.)

By ARTHUR (BUGS) BAER
International News Service columnist

This one is tough to believe.

The Believe It-Or-Not man will not answer the gong Tuesday night.

It rang for the last time Friday afternoon when the incredible Ripley dissolved into the mysterious past whence came his amazing truths.

I spoke to him five minutes before he died. He telephoned me, "I'm in for a check up. I'll be out to your farm tomorrow afternoon."

The Believe It-Or-Not man was a believe it or not himself. Here was a boy from the California hills who never took a drawing lesson in his life. He walked down to San Francisco to be befriended by the great Tad Dorgan, George Herriman and Bob Edgren.

I was talking with Mark Kelly just last week. Mark said, "No wrong guy ever came out of San Francisco," and he was as right as 13 to the dozen.

Ripley and myself were friends for close to 40 years. Both of us landed in New York about the same time. He came through from San Francisco and I was marked perishable freight from Washington.

Rip and I were doubledating on the night he drew his first cartoon. It was a graphic portrayal of odd records in an encyclopedia of athletics. In it was a three legged race, a fellow running backwards, and an ice skater hurdling barrels.

Rip knew if he didn't hurry he would get the one with the thick glasses so he hustled through the drawing and slugged it a careless "Believe It or Not."

That title was to make him ten million dollars. And I got the one with the thick glasses.

That's all anybody had to do with Ripley's success. He was a natural from the jump. He had the pride of craftsmanship in his drawings and the authority of knowledge in his statements. Nobody ever proved him wrong.

If Ripley told me I had two heads I would go out and buy two hats. And tip them both to the greatest cartoonist in the history of American journalism.

LAST PICTURE . . . This photo, taken during his last television program last Tuesday night, shows BOB RIPLEY displaying his collection of crowns worn by the royal families of Europe. Ironically, Ripley, who explained they could be seen at the "Dream House" of N.Y. Heart Association, was a victim of heart disease himself.

Journal-American Photo

Cartoonist Bob Ripley's Burial on Coast Planned

The body of Robert L. Ripley, 55, originator of the world-famous "Believe It or Not," today was reposing in the Abbey Funeral Home, 132 [E. 70th st. He] died yesterday in Harkness Pavilion of Columbia-Presbyterian [Medical Center,] Washington ave. and 168th st.

6—Tues., May 31, 1949 ★★★★ *New York Journal-American*

Leaders in Many Fields Attend Funeral of Ripley

Newspapers, art, sports, aviation and industry were among fields represented by honorary pallbearers at funeral services today for Robert L. Ripley, creator of the internationally known "Believe It or Not" cartoon. Last tribute was paid this afternoon at the Protestant Episcopal Church of St. James, 71st st. and Madison ave.

After the services the body was returned to the Abbel Funeral Home, 132 E. 70th st. Tomorrow evening it will be taken to Santa Rosa, Calif., where final rites will be held at 3 p.m. Saturday at the Odd Fellows' Cemetery.

Over the weekend holiday, thousands of person visited "The Abbey" to pay tribute to Mr. Ripley, who died Friday in the Harkness Pavilion of the [Columbia-Presbyterian Medical Center . . .]

Among the honorary pallbearers were: J. D. Gortatowsky, general manager, Hearst Publications, Inc.; Richard E. Berlin, president, Hearst Corporation; Barry Faris, editor-in-charge, International News Service; Seymour Berkson, vice president and general manager, International News Service; Arthur ...

[*sports columnist:* ...]

[*Daily Mirror;* M. Lincoln Schuster, of the publishing firm of Simon and Schuster; Edward V. Rickenbacker, Gen. James H. Doolittle, Vinnie Richards, Bob Hyland Jr., Earl Dowd; Col. Edward P. F. Eagan ...]

RIPLEY

MOTHER
LILLIE BELLE
1868 – 1915

FATHER
ISAAC D
1854 – 1905

ROBERT L
1890 – 1949

"Believe It or Not"
Ripley

Ripley's Estate Over $1 Million

An estate estimated in excess of $1,000,000 was disposed of in the will of Robert L. Ripley, creator of the famous "Believe It Or Not" cartoons, filed for probate yesterday with Westchester County Surrogate Griffiths in White Plains.

Income of the bulk of the estate, to be placed in trust, will be shared equally by a brother and sister, Douglas Ripley of Mamaroneck and Mrs. Ethel Davis of Burlingame, Cal. After their death the trust is to be terminated and the principal paid to their children.

Mrs. Da[...]
but Dougla[...]
dent of T[...]
Corp., 235[...]
sons, Robe[...]
B, seven m[...]

Bequests[...]
left to 24 f[...]
the largest[...]
est $500.

The $5,000[...]
Li Ling A[...]
Chinese rese[...]
late cartooni[...]
radio agent[...]
sentative; J[...]
friend and[...]
Liese Wisse,[...]
Ming Jung,[...]
William McD[...]
ciate; Cygna[...]
ger, and Pearl[...]
be Norbert[...]
radio adviser.)

Gypsy Mark[...]
dionist and frie[...]
bequeathed $1,0[...]
Edward Eagan,[...]
N. Y. State Ath[...]
and Arthur (Bu[...]
newspaper colu[...]

DOUG STORER is standing on the far right side of the photo.

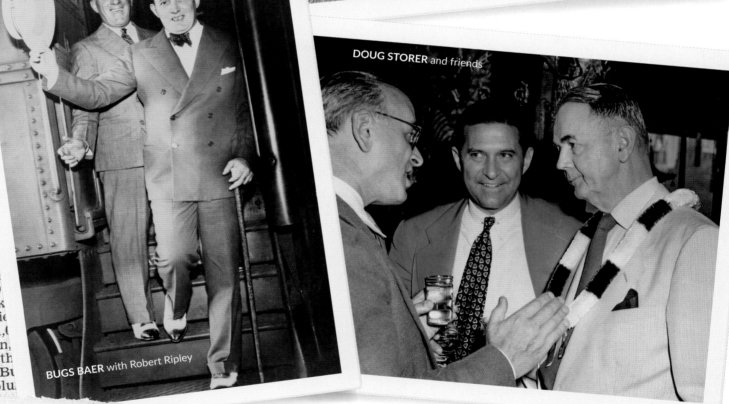

BUGS BAER with Robert Ripley

DOUG STORER and friends

Value Estate Left by Ripley at Over $ Million
Continued from Page 3

Mamaroneck. Like the palatial home, the junk was lavishly ornamented with costly Oriental objects.

Two of the will's witnesses were Reginald Kenny, former captain of the junk, and William L. Platt, present skipper. The third was Liese Wisse, Ripley's personal secretary.

In addition to his Mamaroneck estate, Ripley owned a home at Palm Beach, Fla., and an apartment at 2 W. 67th St.

The will specified that William

P. McCool, 67 Wall St., long associated with Ripley, be retained as counsel for the estate. It was he who filed the document yesterday. Executors and trustees are Robert J. Hyland, Ripley's business manager, and the New York Trust Co., 100 Broadway.

Ripley, 55, died of a heart attack May 27. He was buried at his birthplace, Santa Rosa, Cal., in the Odd Fellows Cemetery.

Bequests not already listed include:

Fella Mellick (an old friend), Trenton,

N. J., $1,000; [...]
and former [...]
Walter St. D[...]
Jermon (oddi[...]
associate); $1,[...]
helped Ripley[...]
Ripley cartoons[...]
associate), $1,0[...]
editor and assis[...]
Features Synd[...]
Ripley cartoons[...]
(editor and sen[...]
tures), $1,000;[...]
friend), $1,000,[...]

Mildred Lodew[...]
Earl Ennis of[...]
largely responsib[...]
first professional[...]
Louise Carter (fri[...]
Greter (artist an[...]
Norwalk, Conn.), [...]

The Mirror[...]
tips. Call MU[...]

$1,000,000 Estate Left by Ripley

The will of Robert L. Ripley, creator of the famed "Believe It or Not" cartoons, was filed for probate today at White Plains with Westchester County Surrogate Charles Griffiths. It deeded the bulk of the cartoonist's estate to a sister and brother, but left bequests of $61,000 to 24 friends and associates.

The total estate is estimated in excess of $1,000,000.

Ripley wrote and stashed his will aboard the Chinese junk *Mon Lei*, where it was found after his death. He bequeathed most of his million-dollar estate to his sister Ethel and brother Doug (who died less than a decade after Ripley).

He also doled out cash awards to specific people in very specific amounts:

- **Bugs Baer**, his close friend for 30 years, received $1,000.

- **Carol Ennis**, a freelance writer who jumpstarted Ripley's career in San Francisco, received $2,500.

- Longtime employees **Norbert Pearlroth** and **Doug Storer** each received $5,000.

- Secretary **William McDonald** and BION Island housekeeper **Jean Doud** each received $5,000.

This page, RIPLEY on the Mon Lei.

MON LEI

里 萬

Where Did It All Go?

The majority of Ripley's artifacts were sold in a four-day-long public auction held three months after his death.

Although his possessions ended up scattered and his family did not continue running the company after 1958, Ripley's Believe It or Not cartoon has taken on a life of its own, evolving into a catchphrase that is still one of the most recognized and used phrases in the English language.

The artifacts sold to John Arthur form the foundation of the Ripley's archives and exhibits that are seen by millions of visitors to the Ripley's Believe It or Not! attractions around the world.

This page, **RIPLEY** with his collection.

The curios and collectibles were rounded up from BION Island, the New York apartment (Nirvana), the Florida house, and the *Mon Lei*.

The lion's share was bought up by New York City entrepreneur John Arthur, who paid out $50,000 of the total $90,000 the auction netted—a fraction of its true value. Arthur also later purchased the *Mon Lei* for another $5,500.

PEOPLE attending the Robert Ripley auction, with a Chinese art importer sitting on the far left. A totem pole (right) from the BION Island property is still owned by Ripley Entertainment.

FORMER song and dance man Harry Richman bidding at Robert Ripley auction.

This page, **AUCTION** books listing every item available from Ripley's massive collection.

People Behind the Man:
A Yearbook

BEATRICE ROBERTS started out as a model before dancing on Broadway in the *Ziegfeld Follies* show, a production that fostered young starlets like Fanny Brice and Bette Davis. Her marriage to Ripley was short-lived.

RIPLEY was best friends with Arthur "Bugs" Baer, a fellow sports cartoonist credited with giving Babe Ruth the nickname "the Sultan of Swat." The two of them romped around New York and competed in citywide handball tournaments.

FOLLOWING the success of the first Ripley book, William Randolph Hearst put Ripley on his payroll. The media mogul paid Ripley $100,000 a year and bankrolled Ripley's travels, which amplified the *Believe It or Not!* brand.

RIPLEY hired Norbert Pearlroth in 1923 as a part-time linguist and translator, but he soon became the man behind the cartoon curtain. Pearlroth's expertise and researching capabilities made him a lifelong partner. Ripley later described him as a "walking encyclopedia."

RUTH ROSS was a young, vivacious woman who grew into Ripley's travel companion, employee, and lover. (Ross was married to another man.)

Robert Ripley's **FATHER**, Isaac Davis Ripley.

Robert Ripley's **MOTHER**, Lillie Belle Yucca.

Above, **RIPLEY'S** younger brother, Douglas, refused to come live with Ripley for many years, preferring a nomadic lifestyle, but he reluctantly came to work with his brother in 1931. Never comfortable with Ripley's lifestyle and the business side of things, Doug left the company to Storer in the 1950s.

Above, **DOUG STORER** started as a radio show promoter and helped Ripley make some noise on the platform before becoming president of Ripley's Believe It or Not! after Ripley's death.

Right, **CHINESE** American Li Ling Ai charmed Ripley with her elegance, wit, and beauty. An actress, author, and lecturer, she became a fixture at BION Island and Ripley's New York apartment. She was his steadfast friend up until his death in 1949.

the **MAN**

the **COLLECTION**

the **TRAVELS**

the **CARTOONS**

the **MEDIA**

the **LOCATIONS**

the **COMPANY**

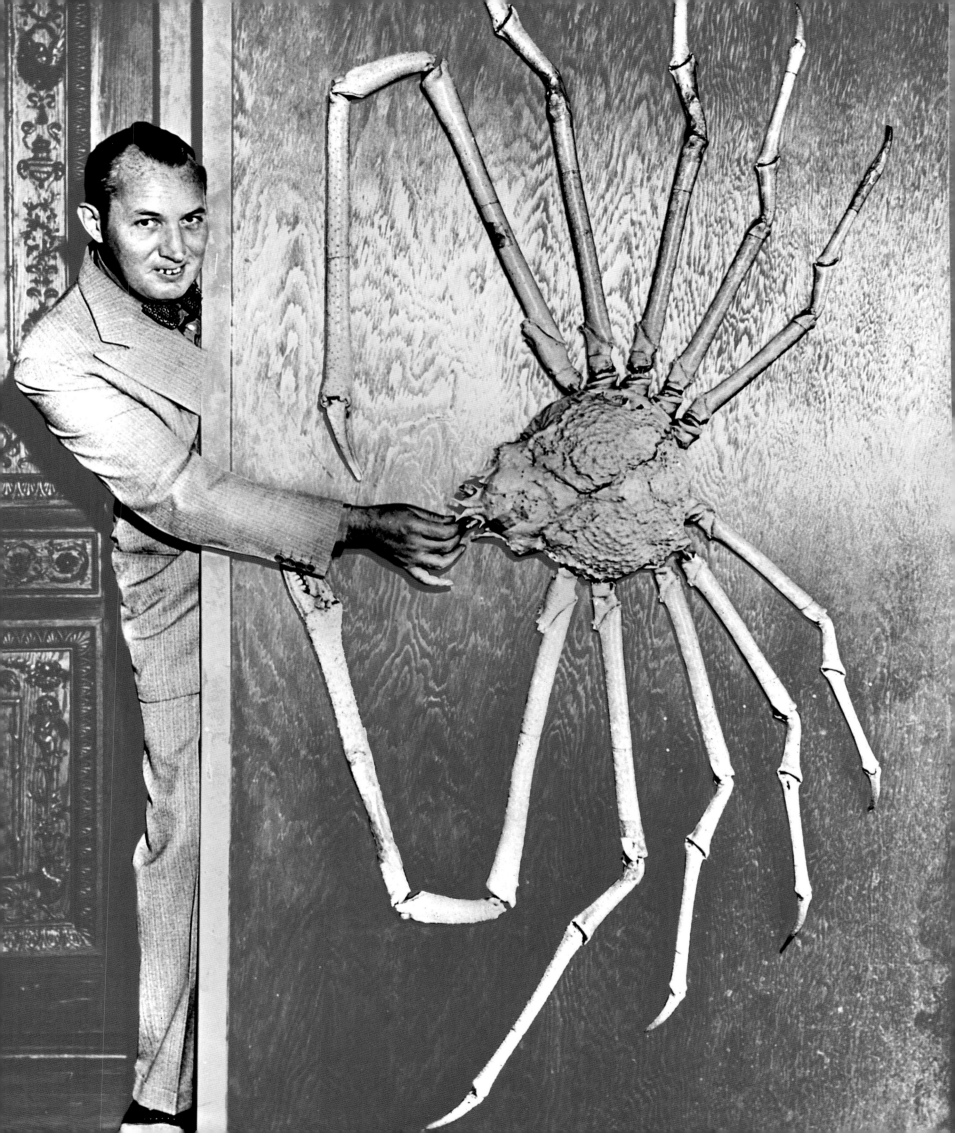

The Collection

"This company is the only place I've ever worked full time, as I started directly out of college."

—Edward Meyer, previous VP of Exhibits and Archives

Foreword by Edward Meyer

During my 33 years as VP of Exhibits and Archives I have seen it all—and bought most of it, too! I am still like a kid in a candy shop, always excited about the next best thing.

Robert Ripley started collecting artifacts sometime around 1925. Initially, the items were brought back from his travels, as he visited 201 countries between 1913 and 1940. By the time he bought his first house in 1934 (a palatial 28-room mansion on an island in Mamaroneck, New York), he already had enough things to fill it as well as his first Odditorium in Chicago. When Ripley died in 1949, he left behind three houses full of artifacts, and in total, there were three separate auctions held for Ripley's valuable possessions.

Ripley's very first purchase was a genuine Jivaro (or Shuar) shrunken head from Ecuador—a classic Believe It or Not! icon. The first item I bought, on the other hand, was a small piece of tanned skin from a 19th-century murderer, inscribed by surgeon Richard Smith who dissected him after he was hung for his crime.

A colleague brought the newspaper clipping to me, and everyone thought it was a great story for the cartoon, which it was, but I was determined to actually buy the skin. I still think it's a great piece more than 30 years later. This is one I would go buy today if it came across my desk again. It was certainly a memorable beginning to a long career.

I began working for Ripley's in May 1978 for the summer to catalog the Ripley's newspaper cartoon. At that point, Alec Rigby had already owned the company for eight years, and the newspaper cartoon was still kept in boxes. I went back to school in the fall, working on a master's degree, when out of the blue, Alec Rigby offered me a part-time job. I was going to school during the day and working two or three hours at Ripley's each night. Eventually, he offered me a full-time position, and I quit school.

With Jimmy Pattison's acquisition of the company in 1985, growth became the mantra, although it soon became evident that to fuel that growth, we needed more exhibits. There had been odds and ends bought for local, site-specific interest for new Odditoriums, but fundamentally, there was no one buying artifacts from 1949 to 1985.

Above, **EDWARD** posing with a shrunken head.

My job changed overnight, and exhibit acquisition became my main focus. We determined that we had to buy 500 items a year because that's how many go on display in a museum. At our peak, we were buying as many as 1,200 items annually, which is four a day every week day of the year.

The largest thing I ever bought was a 45-foot-long whale skeleton—actually I've bought two, both of which are now displayed in our aquariums in Gatlinburg and Toronto. As for my personal favorites, I'm still amazed by the Lord's Prayer engraved on the head of a pin. It is believed seven of these exist, although ours is the only one that's flawless. Miniatures appeal to me because I can't fathom how they are done. I love all of our exhibits, and they have all shaped our collection in some way or another.

"I'm incredibly indebted to Bob Masterson, longtime president of Ripley's, who had the faith to let me loose on the world and the confidence that I would find and buy artifacts of interest and lasting value."

— Edward Meyer

This page, **EDWARD** on an elephant during a trip to Thailand.

The Collection

Of course, there's been some changes over the years. We don't spend our money on the same kind of the things we used to—antiquities to some extent have been replaced with pop culture memorabilia. The percentage of exhibits bought at auction has gone up. Historically, it was 1 percent, and then we got into the history auction business and it went up closer to 10 percent. Then we got into pop culture and it doubled to 20 percent. However, I still think the best things in the Ripley collection find us.

Based on the items bought by John Arthur at the first estate auction, roughly 3,000 artifacts made up the original Ripley collection, including a full-size authentic Chinese junk called the *Mon Lei*. Today, the Ripley collection fills 30 Odditoriums and a 22,000-square-foot warehouse in Central Florida. We have more than 25,000 items, not counting more than 125,000 original pen-and-ink drawings by Ripley and the six successive cartoon artists since his death.

No doubt what we add to our collection in our second 100 years will diversify and change with the times. We will always, however, in the great tradition of our founder Robert L. Ripley, continue to acquire and display the strange, the odd, the unbelievable with an eye to entertaining and educating a whole new generation of Believe It or Not! fans.

Below, **EDWARD** with a Colombian beaded mask at the Orlando warehouse.

Above, **EDWARD** with the Marilyn Monroe gown, the World's Most Expensive Dress!

PETRIFIED CORPSE

EDWARD, with his two-tone beard, meeting Jimmy Carter at a company function in 1995.

This page, **EDWARD** with a mummified Chicago circus sideshow performer from the 1920s. The mummy continued to "work" for the circus after death, displayed as an authentic Egyptian mummy.

What We Collect

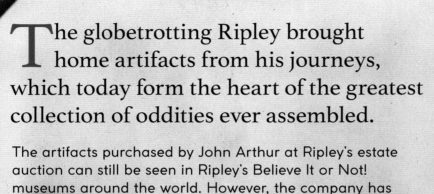

The globetrotting Ripley brought home artifacts from his journeys, which today form the heart of the greatest collection of oddities ever assembled.

The artifacts purchased by John Arthur at Ripley's estate auction can still be seen in Ripley's Believe It or Not! museums around the world. However, the company has come a long way since Ripley lugged crates of curios back to his homes.

With the addition of a dedicated exhibit buyer in the mid-1980s, the company began expanding the scope of the collection. Cannibal skulls, Chinese lily slippers, and shrunken heads are all displayed alongside exhibits like jars of belly button lint or a Twizzler dress.

Everything in the collection must meet the following criteria in order to be included: it should be shocking, fascinating, bizarre, or all of the above.

"Most of the exhibits in the early attractions date all the way back to the World's Fair in Chicago and then came out of the New York show that was on Broadway, which was still there when I started."

—Bob Masterson, former Ripley's president

Above, ROBERT RIPLEY standing at his BION Island home bar next to North American and West African totem statues, circa 1939.

JOHN ARTHUR standing with his treasures from the Robert Ripley auction, including a mammoth beer stein and an Iron Maiden spiked torture device.

Left, DRESS made out of licorice Twizzlers.

Above, SHRUNKEN HEAD from the Ripley's Vault.

BION Island

Ripley's museum-like homes, two in New York and eventually one in Florida, were stuffed with artifacts and curios. One could say the first museums were his own houses.

Treasures like the ones listed here were displayed throughout Ripley's BION Island home:

- Brass, gilded, and wooden Buddha sculptures

- African idols

- Spears, masks, torture devices, shields, and pieces of armor adorning the walls

- Japanese carved bone ceremonial sword

- Flags from every country he'd visited

- Skin vase lamp

- Eskimo whale harpoons

- Eskimo stein made of walrus tooth

- Two mammoth tusks

- Oriental Soochow jade lamp

- Italian Renaissance carved ivory helmet

- English porcelain wine barrel

- Ming-period brass temple gong

- Jawbone of a man-eating shark

- Petrified snake in a velvet case

- Shrunken human heads from Ecuador

- African Congo funeral masks

- Jesse James's gun

- Whale ear

- Finger-bone necklace

This page, **RIPLEY** in front of his BION Island home in winter.

His palatial 28-room home in Mamaroneck, New York—BION Island, short for "believe it or not"—housed hundreds of Chinese statues and wall hangings, Native American totem poles, a huge collection of beer steins, weapons of torture from Germany, and colossal Oriental bronze guardian statues.

RIPLEY in his Manhattan apartment among all his treasures.

RIPLEY'S BION Island home bed.

ORIENTAL cabinets and sculptures inside Ripley's home.

RIPLEY in front of one of the totem poles at BION Island.

Ripley had installed a giant compass on the grounds of BION Island. Each spoke pointed to places he had been, listing the names of cities and the distances to them from BION Island.

Mon Lei

Ever the Sinophile, Ripley purchased his favorite getaway in 1946—a Chinese junk called the *Mon Lei*.

Built in 1939 for a wealthy Hong Kong businessman, whom Ripley always referred to as a "war lord," the ship was a 50-foot-long fishing boat known as a "junk." Ripley quickly sunk $40,000 to restore the worn-out vessel.

In recognition of nautical Chinese beliefs and superstitions, he did no less than the following:

- Painted eyes, teeth, and whiskers on the new diesel engine (in response to the Chinese belief that boats are propelled by the spirits of dragons)

- Hid the engine behind a gilded altar to the Chinese god of joy, Ho Tei

- Painted every available space with traditional Chinese sailing proverbs

- Chose the entwined yin and yang symbols for the boat's flag

- Installed a gong (to ward off evil spirits)

- Gold-plated the anchor (because Chinese sailors believed that only a golden anchor could hold fast)

- Used gold and red lacquer for the overall paint scheme

- Maintained a flashy Mandarin wardrobe aboard for his guests

- Kept the name *Mon Lei* (which means "10,000 miles" or "infinity" in Chinese)

Ripley effectively converted the ship into one of the most amazing pleasure yachts in America. He sailed up and down the East Coast and would invite friends aboard for weekend floating parties complete with cocktails and Chinese food.

The Ripley Entertainment global empire today remarkably does not include the *Mon Lei*. After Ripley's death, it was purchased by John Arthur, who then quickly sold it.

Below, ROBERT RIPLEY and his guests are shown aboard his colorful Chinese junk enjoying a game of mahjong before starting on a cruise on the Long Island Sound.

Above, THE MON LEI pictured in one of Ripley's few color paintings, dated 1948.

Above, THIS WOODEN MODEL of the Mon Lei, painstakingly restored by Ripley's own artist Bruce Miller, was a gift to Robert Ripley in the 1940s.

Above, RIPLEY decorated the Mon Lei with many of his treasures, including this intricately carved wood paneling.

Masakichi Statue

Prominently featured in world's fair Odditoriums and the Ripley's Mobile Museum, the Masakichi statue was another of Ripley's favorites.

The exhibit is a life-size self-portrait of Japanese artist Hananuma Masakichi. The artist created his own image for his fiancée after learning he was dying of tuberculosis. The sculpture, consisting of hundreds of tiny interlocking pieces of wood skillfully dovetailed and joined to avoid detection, is anatomically correct down to the smallest detail and includes the artist's own hair, fingernails, and teeth.

Ripley loved to play pranks with it, such as hiding the nude Masakichi statue in closets where house guests were staying and then waiting outside to listen for their shouts of terror.

The Masakichi statue, still an active part of the collection, is currently on display at the Amsterdam Odditorium.

BELIEVE IT OR NOT Ripley

THE ODDITORIUM IN THE HEART OF NEW YORK CITY AT 48th STREET AND BROADWAY

Left, **ARTICLE** on Masakichi with photo of Ripley and exhibit.

Below, **A POSTCARD** of the Masakichi statue as seen in the store Ripley bought it from in 1934. Photo was taken circa the 1910–20s at The House of Novelties and Curios in San Francisco, California.

© BION

This statue is but one of hundreds of curiosities, souvenirs, relics and oddities gathered from all parts of the world and on exhibition at

The HOUSE OF NOVELTIES AND CURIOS
E. Bloch Mercantile Company
70 Market Street — San Francisco, Cal.

MASAKICHI, the man.

THE JAPANESE MAN

THIS Oriental image is so realistic in detail that it seems the man himself stands there in flesh and blood. And such was the artist's intention! It was carved by Hananuma Masakichi, the illustrious Japanese artist, as a reproduction of himself.

Mr. Ripley avers this is the most lifelike image ever made by man. He searched the world over for this statue for 20 years and finally found it in a small Oriental curio shop.

Over 2,000 pieces of wood were used in it. The body is made of hundreds of pieces or strips glued together—no nails, screws or metals were used. Made in Yokohama in 1885, it shows the artist at the age of 53. Hananuma, suffering from tuberculosis, realized that his end was near and sought to leave a monument of himself. The result is undoubtedly the greatest work of art of its kind ever done.

An exact counterpart of the artist, the size is the same, the pose, the features, the skin is the same color and apparent texture, the hair is the same, the blue veins, the muscles, the prominent collarbones, the tubercular hollows in the neck, the outlines of the ribs, even the hairs adorning the figure. Each separate hair was plucked from his own body and inserted—one by one—in holes bored for them. He took out his own teeth and put them inside the mouth. He removed his own finger-nails and toe-nails and fixed them on the figure. The eyes were made of glass by Hananuma himself and are a wonder of the optical profession, so human and alive are they. Finally, Masakichi added his own carving tools, loin cloth and spectacles, and in his will left all of his worldly goods to his image.

Strange and fascinating, this figure symbolizes the curious facts assembled by Robert L. Ripley of "Believe It or Not" fame which we are bringing to you the coming twelve months. This folder is the first, the other eleven following at monthly intervals.

Please accept them with our compliments and let them be a reminder of our desire to be of service.

RIPLEY BELIEVE IT OR NOT, INC., NEW YORK, N

Fiji Mermaid

Believe it or not, one of Ripley's favorite exhibits helped make P. T. Barnum a household name—and it just so happened to be a fake!

In 1842, P. T. Barnum was approached by a man who offered him a preserved mermaid, which he leased for $12.50 a week. Soon afterward, New York newspapers ran stories on the amazing mummified mermaid obtained from the little-known Fiji Islands. The papers and the public bought the deception completely. Barnum moved the mermaid to his American museum and then throughout the United States for his standard 25-cent admission fee, nearly tripling his business and launching his circus career.

Barnum insisted his "Fiji Mermaid" was genuine until in his old age, when he admitted that the "mermaid" was just a fusing of the upper half of a monkey and the lower half of a fish.

Above, **VINTAGE** ad for the Fiji mermaid.

"Barnum was wrong. The public doesn't like to be fooled. And I'm happy to say I've never fooled my public. Not that the public always thinks so."

—Robert Ripley

Left, **BRANDISHING** a Fiji mermaid, Ripley startles an usherette at the New York City Odditorium in 1939.

Below, **A PORTRAIT** of P. T. Barnum.

WORLD'S GREATEST FAKE

IN 1842, THE NEW YORK HERALD PRINTED A REPORT THAT DR. J. GRIFFIN OF THE 'LONDON LYCEUM OF NATURAL HISTORY' HAD PASSED THROUGH MONTGOMERY, ALABAMA WITH A MOST REMARKABLE CURIOSITY — A VERITABLE FIJI ISLAND MERMAID. THE ODDITY WAS PURCHASED IN CALCUTTA IN 1817 FOR £6,000 — IT IS ACTUALLY A MONKEY'S HEAD AND CHEST, CLEVERLY SEWN TO A FISH'S BODY.

DR. GRIFFIN WAS A FAKE AND SO WAS THE MERMAID. THE WHOLE THING WAS ONE OF P. T. BARNUM'S GREAT HOAXES. WHEN THE FIJI MERMAID WAS FIRST DISPLAYED AT BARNUM'S AMERICA MUSEUM IN 1843 HUNDREDS OF PEOPLE LINED UP TO SEE IT AT 25¢ A PEEP.

Shrunken Heads

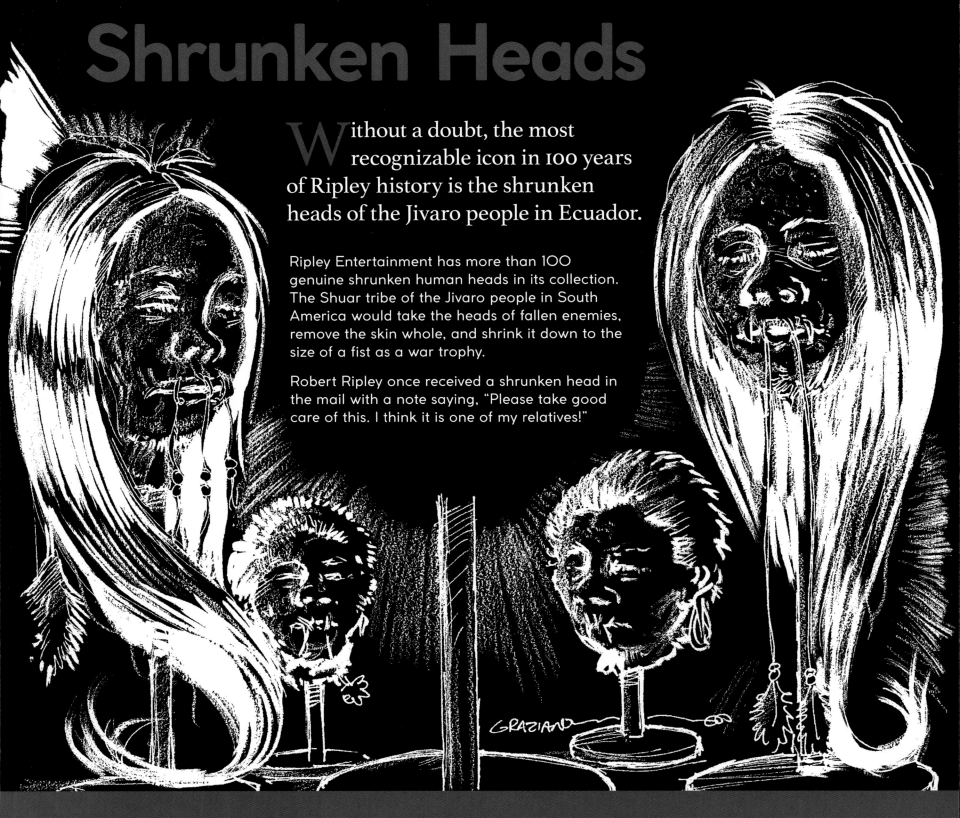

Without a doubt, the most recognizable icon in 100 years of Ripley history is the shrunken heads of the Jivaro people in Ecuador.

Ripley Entertainment has more than 100 genuine shrunken human heads in its collection. The Shuar tribe of the Jivaro people in South America would take the heads of fallen enemies, remove the skin whole, and shrink it down to the size of a fist as a war trophy.

Robert Ripley once received a shrunken head in the mail with a note saying, "Please take good care of this. I think it is one of my relatives!"

Most people do not know there are three types of shrunken heads:

1. **Tsantsas**

2. **Non-ceremonial human heads**

3. **False heads**

Tsantsas are authentic Jivaro-produced ceremonial human shrunken heads. They have a narrower face, very dark skin, and almost vertical nostrils.

Real but **non-ceremonial** shrunken heads were made for the tourist trade. The "souvenir" shrunken heads were made to retain realistic proportions dictated by the demands of tourists more concerned with human-looking shrunken heads than authenticity.

False heads are imitations made from molded animal skin. They tend to lack detail: the mouth is just a slit with ridges, the ears have no structure or even a hole, and the hair is glued on. They are also much lighter in weight than the real ones.

Left, **RIPLEY** holds a shrunken head with long hair at the New York City Odditorium, circa 1939. He acquired the head in the 1920s, but it dates back to the 1800s.

Below, **A VERY** rare shrunken female torso (one of six known to exist) at one time owned by Ernest Hemingway. Since traditionally the Jivaro did not shrink female heads (shrunken heads are war trophies, and women traditionally didn't go to war), this torso was probably prepared in the early 20th century, deliberately to sell to tourists.

Above, **POSSIBLY** a Caucasian male, decorated with parrot feather.

A Selection of the Collection

Fertility Statues. Hand carved by Baulé tribesman from ebony wood in the 1930s, each statue stands 5 feet tall and weighs more than 70 pounds. The set includes a male and female, with the woman holding a baby and the man holding a mango and a dagger—symbols of fertility. The statues are meant to be placed on either side of a bedroom doorway. Legend says that a woman and her spouse hoping to conceive should touch the statues as they enter the room. These statues have traveled around the world to every Odditorium three times since 1996!

Left, **THE LORD'S PRAYER** on the head of a pin. Convicted forger A. Schiller created six pins with the Lord's Prayer, only revealed under magnification, engraved on each. There is a single perfect specimen, a gold pin 47/1000ths of an inch in diameter, and this is the pin on display in Odditoriums today.

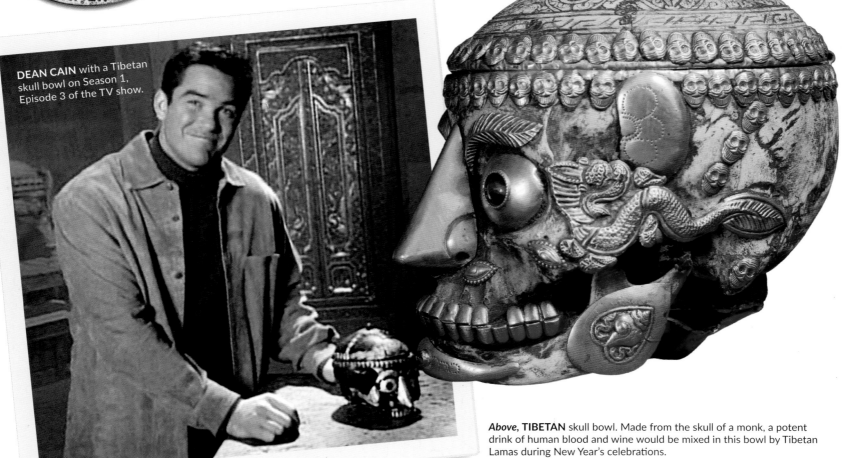

DEAN CAIN with a Tibetan skull bowl on Season 1, Episode 3 of the TV show.

Above, **TIBETAN** skull bowl. Made from the skull of a monk, a potent drink of human blood and wine would be mixed in this bowl by Tibetan Lamas during New Year's celebrations.

Ripley's boasts a large and varied taxidermy collection, although the most shocking animals tend to have polycephaly (the condition of having more than one head) or polymelia (the condition of having more than the usual number of limbs). They are the product of conjoined twins, and often these animals don't live long after birth.

THREE-LEGGED Duck

SIX-LEGGED Zebra

TWO-HEADED Calf

Edward Meyer gives some context for the pieces of the Berlin Wall in the Ripley's collection:

Norm Deska, myself, Bob Masterson, and Sylvia Makiko—who was our vice president of operations at the time and of German descent—went to Hamburg, Germany, to see a collection that Bob had discovered. After our business in Hamburg, we drove to Berlin on the Autobahn. We had a little tiny Mercedes that we kept at 130 mph and got passed by everybody honking their horns because we were apparently going too slow.

We arrived three days after the Wall fell. We went with an empty suitcase, a Swiss army knife, and a hammer, and I loaded it up with pieces the size of your fist. There were probably thousands of people taking pieces of the Berlin Wall, and suddenly the light bulb went off in my head, and I said, "Why are we taking handfuls? Let's take a big piece." With Sylvia as a translator, we were able to broker a deal and take much larger sections of the Wall.

It was expensive to truck it from Berlin back to Hamburg, and then it came across from Hamburg to America by ship.

I would say it's probably my proudest moment. In my opinion, I think it is the single biggest event of the 20th century, both the building of the wall in the first place and then certainly the fall of the wall. It clearly changed Germany forever.

The pieces have been a wonderful historical addition to our collection.

"We have 160 feet of the Berlin Wall—
sixteen 10-foot sections—and we hand-
picked the pieces that had the best graffiti."
—Edward Meyer

Above, **WOOD** fantasy coffin, styled as a leopard, 8.75 feet long.

Above and left, **WOOD** fantasy coffin, styled as a white Mercedes Benz.

The Ga people of Ghana, Africa, often order designer hand-carved fantasy coffins that reflect the occupation, status, or achievements of the deceased.

Chinese Lily Slippers. In ancient China, daughters of wealthy families purposely broke and bound their feet. The ideal foot was 3 inches long and was crushed into a shape resembling a lotus flower.

A BOUND FOOT. This diagram shows the twisted and cramped bone structure of a bound ("lily") foot, as compared with that of a normal foot. Bound tightly with cloth from the age of five, a little girl's foot grew painfully into this deformed but erotically admired shape.

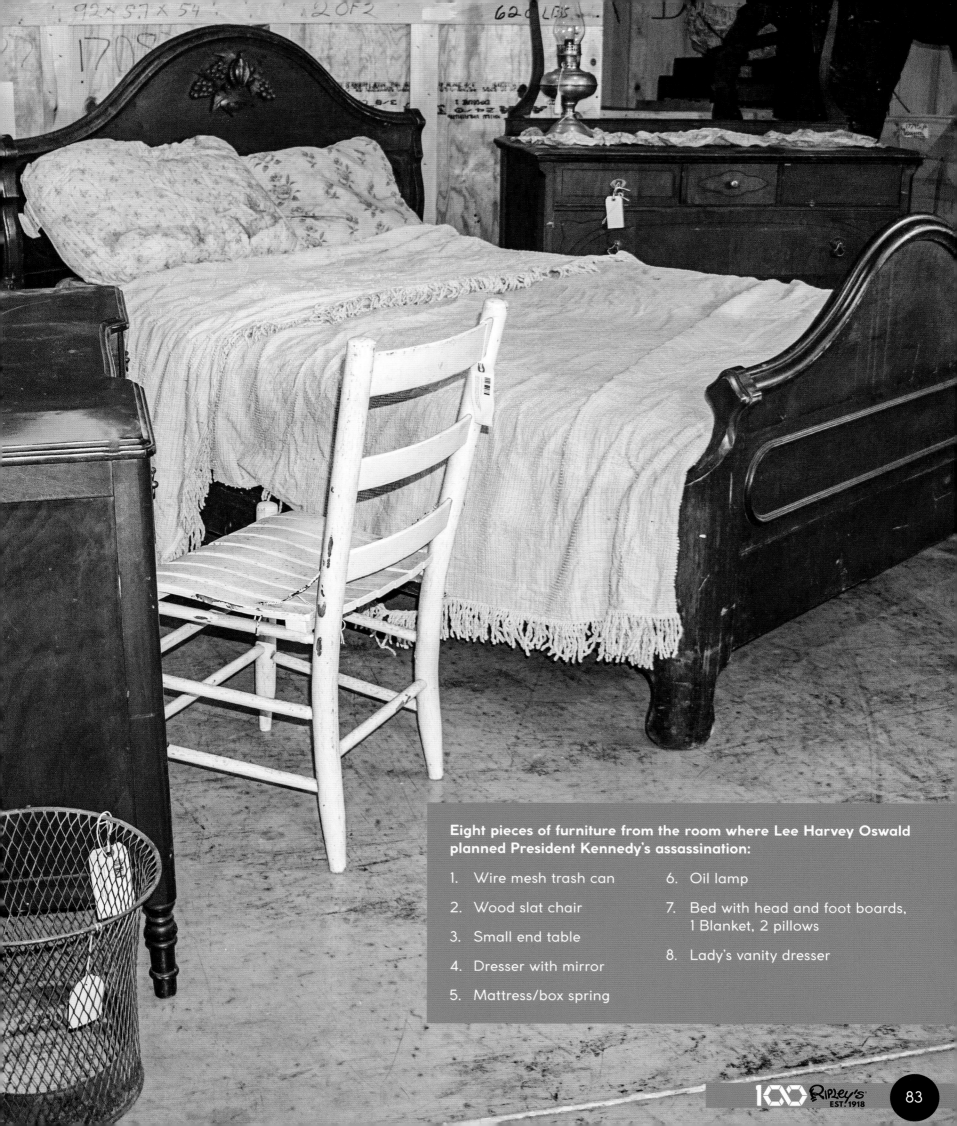

Eight pieces of furniture from the room where Lee Harvey Oswald planned President Kennedy's assassination:

1. Wire mesh trash can
2. Wood slat chair
3. Small end table
4. Dresser with mirror
5. Mattress/box spring
6. Oil lamp
7. Bed with head and foot boards, 1 Blanket, 2 pillows
8. Lady's vanity dresser

Above, ROAD TO ODD by Jeff Hanson. This 5-feet-wide acrylic piece is painted on heavily textured and woven canvas with sisal rope. Hanson's vision is impaired from an optic nerve tumor related to neurofibromatosis. He still creates works of art despite his visual impairment. *Odd Is Art* Ripley's collection contributor.

Above, GEISHA WOMAN by James Butman. Featuring a geisha under a cherry tree, the piece was created with 5,000 postage stamps as therapy for the artist's agoraphobia, or fear of public places.

Below, THE LINT SUPPER by Laura Bell. Leonardo Da Vinci's *The Last Supper* recreated with laundry lint. The artist dried specific pieces of clothing in order to obtain the correct colors of lint.

Found in Zagami, Africa, in 1963, this piece of a meteorite contains gases not found anywhere on Earth. Unidentifiable until NASA recovered soil and rock samples from Mars, the origin of the meteorite was a mystery. Now, however, scientists are certain the Zagami meteorite is in fact a 9-million-year-old piece of the planet Mars.

Edward Meyer recounted the purchase of the Mars meteorite:

We have three really good friends in New York City: one deals with bones, one deals with skins, and one deals with meteorites, and they're all best buddies. We were at an auction of meteorites in New York City when we were approached by a guy who asked us if we would be interested in a Martian meteorite. Our friend, who is one of the most renowned meteorite guys in the country, basically brokered the deal and verified that the meteorite was indeed from Mars.

That is the number one meteorite in the world, and we bought it. It was more than we'd ever paid for meteorite, but it wasn't sky-high—no pun intended. We bought the one whole piece for about $50,000. Today it's insured for about $5,000,000.

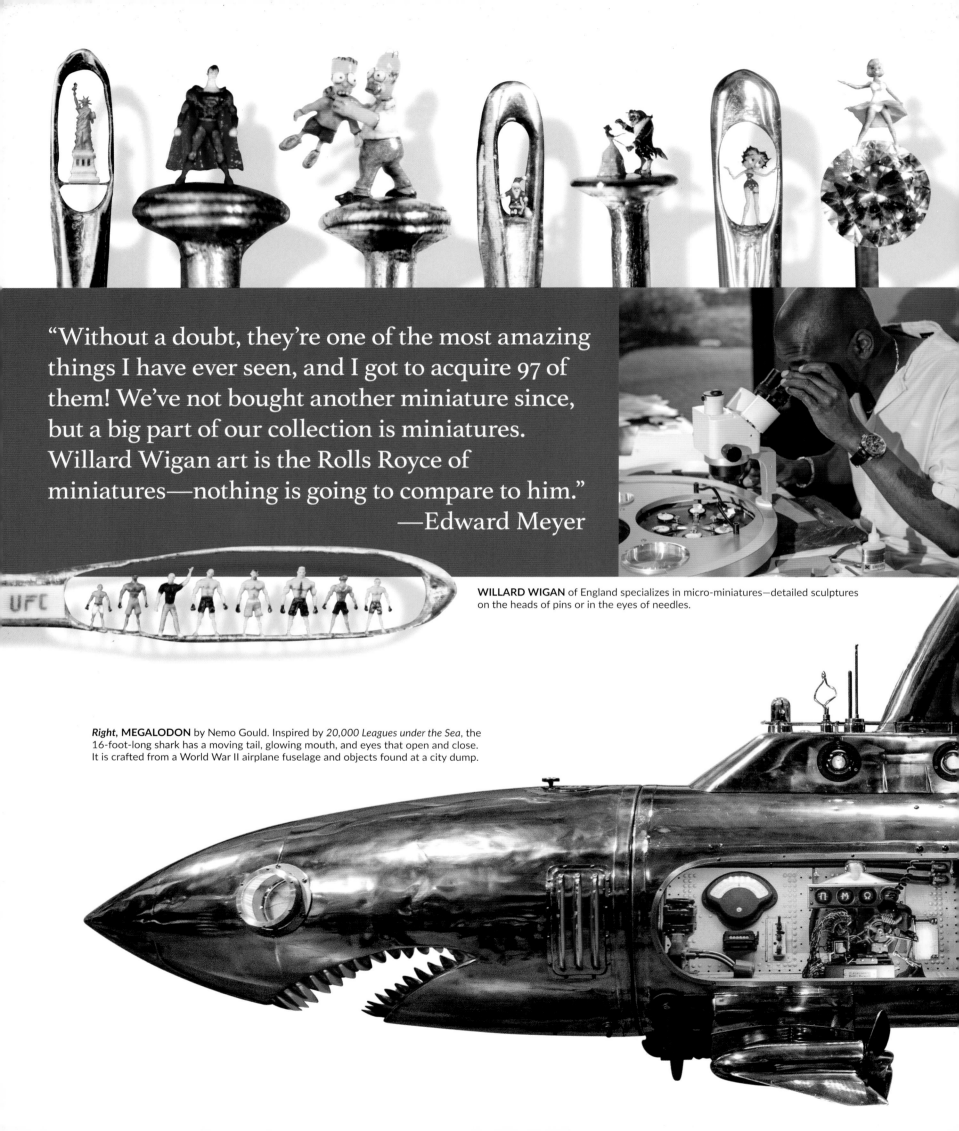

"Without a doubt, they're one of the most amazing things I have ever seen, and I got to acquire 97 of them! We've not bought another miniature since, but a big part of our collection is miniatures. Willard Wigan art is the Rolls Royce of miniatures—nothing is going to compare to him."
—Edward Meyer

WILLARD WIGAN of England specializes in micro-miniatures—detailed sculptures on the heads of pins or in the eyes of needles.

Right, **MEGALODON** by Nemo Gould. Inspired by *20,000 Leagues under the Sea*, the 16-foot-long shark has a moving tail, glowing mouth, and eyes that open and close. It is crafted from a World War II airplane fuselage and objects found at a city dump.

Below, a life-sized recreation of James Bond's car as seen in the movies *Goldfinger* and *Thunderball* made completely out of recycled cardboard and glue.

BMT 216A

BMT 216A

IN 1985, John Lennon's psychedelic Rolls-Royce Phantom V was purchased at auction for $2.29 million, the highest amount paid for a car at that time. After its display at Expo 86, the car was donated for a Victoria, BC, museum exhibit in 1987. Believe it or not, after its donation, a priceless never-before-seen home movie was found behind the back seat.

Above, **RUSSELL POWELL** is able to paint an incredible amount of detail onto his palm before pressing it onto a canvas, creating palm paintings. Using multiple stampings, he created this collage of inspirational and famous guitarists. *Odd Is Art* Ripley's collection contributor.

HOGWARTS Castle from *Harry Potter* made from 500,000+ matchsticks, by Patrick Acton.

Above, **ORIGINAL** lightsaber used by Mark Hamill (Luke Skywalker) in the first two Star Wars films, *A New Hope* and *The Empire Strikes Back*.

Above, **FRANKENSTEIN** monster made from keyboard keys by artist Doug Powell.

Above, **PAINTED** Tarantula by Jesus Lopez. One in a series of 10 painted tarantulas featuring Spider-Man battling against some of his arch enemies.

This page, **KING KONG** gorilla figure made entirely from strips of recycled tires. Measuring more than 13 feet tall and weighing nearly one ton, it was made in Thailand.

The Marilyn Dress

At the expense and urging of Jimmy Pattison, Ripley's bought Marilyn Monroe's "Happy Birthday, Mr. President" dress at auction for a record $4.8 million.

The iconic dress was famously worn by Monroe on May 19, 1962, when she sang "Happy Birthday" to President John F. Kennedy at Madison Square Garden. Covered in thousands of rhinestones, the dress was so tight, it's said that Monroe had to be sewn into it.

Although Monroe (whose real name was Norma Jeane Mortenson) died tragically at the young age of 36, her charisma, filmography, and status as a sex symbol has made her an enduring pop culture phenomenon.

Throughout the years, Ripley Entertainment has purchased numerous pieces of Marilyn memorabilia and tours the items as a traveling exhibit in the Odditoriums, allowing guests to get as close as possible to the legendary star.

Right, A FOX stole owned by Marilyn.

Below, RING worn by Marilyn Monroe in the film *Gentlemen Prefer Blondes*.

Above, THE DRESS was designed by Jean Louis, a French-born Hollywood costume designer, but the original sketch of the dress showing Monroe in the nearly nude gown was done by none other than a 22-year-old Bob Mackie in his first job out of college. In an interview, he mentioned that he took some inspiration from "dresses where you could see through but not see anything." Bob Mackie went on to dress entertainment icons such as Cher, Bette Midler, Diana Ross, and Judy Garland.

Edward explains the Marilyn dress auction process:

The most expensive thing I ever bought was a dress worn by Marilyn Monroe to sing "Happy Birthday" to then-president John F. Kennedy. I almost bought it in 1999 in New York for a million dollars, but didn't get it until 2016 when it cost us $4.81 million—just a bit of inflation in 17 years.

After seeing the catalog and ad, I called Jimmy Pattison (the owner of Ripley's), and he was very excited. He knew instantly what I was talking about.

We were going to take a run at this dress—that's auction verbiage.

However, when Jimmy's interested, there's no run; he is going to buy it. But he didn't want to spend $5 million on it. I landed in L.A. about two hours before the auction. I phoned Jimmy and he says we're not going to spend $5,000,000. I was just totally deflated. All the excitement gone.

It was the last item of the evening, so I sat there for a couple hours before it came time to bid.

The bidding started at a million and went up by a $100,000 to $2,000,000, in just 10 bids, boom, boom, boom, boom. It took like one second. The initial pause now at $2,000,000 because now it's going to go up by $500,000. I tell Jimmy it's *not* ours at $2.5 million. "Bid," he says. Now we're at $3,000,000. The room is relatively quiet. They start the "going once, going twice, going three times" and drag that out. They get the $3.5 million and Jimmy has lost the dress. It may have been the first time I've ever been with Jimmy that he paused.

He eventually says bid, so it's mine at $4,000,000. The head of Julian's is close by, looking me in the face. The paparazzi is now all behind me. After two minutes of the auction staff talking, the dress is ours for $5 million. The whole thing took 7 minutes—4½ of that is them talking, so it's really a 2½-minute deal to spend more than $5,000,000 after all taxes and fees.

It's over so quickly, there's no time to dwell on your nerves. I was up doing interviews till three in the morning. I got about two hours of sleep before the interviews from Europe started. We were still doing interviews at four in the afternoon, so it was about 16 hours of media. It was just amazing—and we still had to get up and go to the auction on day 2 to buy some more stuff!

Julien's AUCTIONS
THE AUCTION HOUSE TO THE STARS
572

The Warehouse

When not on display or in need of repair, exhibits are housed in the Ripley's warehouse in Orlando, Florida.

Below, **THE LOOK** and feel of the Ripley's warehouse has been mimicked in many Odditoriums, with the addition of a warehouse-themed section.

Below, **THE LOOK** and feel of the Ripley's warehouse has been mimicked in many Odditoriums, with the addition of a warehouse-themed section.

This page, **RIPLEY'S** warehouse in Orlando, Florida.

Khabli Skull Bowl

Believe It or Not!, the bowl shown before you was made from the skull of a Tibetan monk and used during New Year's celebrations to mix a...

In 2014, Edward purchased a tiger hairball meant to be an exhibit, but alas...

It's almost not an item because we didn't have it very long.

I was watching the morning news and I heard that this veterinarian/owner was trying to raise money to save a tiger. Basically, the tiger was going to die because they didn't have the money to operate—it was choking on a giant basketball-sized hairball. We gave them the money so they could operate and save the tiger's life. They were very grateful, but I said, "Well, you know, what's a tiger hairball look like?" Maybe a week later, the hairball was delivered from Tampa, Florida. It didn't look pretty (it looked like vomit), and it smelled like hell. We thought, *That's not something we can display as is.*

While we were deciding what to do with it, we put it outside to get the smell out of the office. It was in our beer cooler at the back of the warehouse underneath the stairs, within probably three feet of the door. It was there no more than an hour when we went out to show somebody our smelly purchase and the cooler was gone. We can only imagine what happened when the people thinking they were stealing our beer cooler opened it up. They wouldn't know what it was—they'd just get the smell.

Above, **TIGER** that was saved from a giant hairball.

Left, **THE HAIRBALL** that was removed from the tiger.

The Art Department

R ipley Entertainment's in-house art department studio is located alongside the warehouse, where artists bring Odditorium props and all-true stories and unbelievable people to life.

Historical BIONs and new additions to the Ripley family don't find their way into Odditoriums and Louis Tussaud's Waxworks without first being rendered and often hand-sculpted by in-house staff. The Ripley artists make display figures based on archival photos and video footage, as well as from castings of contemporary celebrities and Ripley talent.

Below, **ROBERT WADLOW** (1918–40), the tallest man ever to have lived, stood 8 feet 11 inches tall and wore size 37 shoes that cost $100 a pair—equivalent to $1,500 today. Like most excessively tall people, he had suffered from an over-active pituitary gland, which resulted in an abnormally high level of human growth hormone.

Left, **J. T. SAYLORS** from Georgia first demonstrated his talent for contorting his face into a funny expression (a.k.a. gurning) at the first Ripley's Odditorium in Chicago in 1933.

OLD FUNNY FACE!

J.T. SAYLORS - of Villa Rica Ga. CAN DISLOCATE HIS JAWS AND SWALLOW HIS NOSE

Above, JOHN CENA sculpture made of silicone being assembled by art department artist Brent Gothold.

MARIA undergoing a body cast of her face.

MARIA Jose Cristerna, a.k.a. the Vampire Woman, having her teeth measured.

Above, FEATURED in Ripley's 2012 Download the Weird, Maria Jose Cristerna has completed extensive body modifications.

THE COMPLETED resin figure.

THE RESIN FIGURE of Brittany Walsh, a.k.a. Acrobritt, being painted by art department artist Ashli Szymanski-Combs.

Above, KAYAN women of Myanmar (formerly Burma) are known as "long-neck women" because of the custom of placing heavy brass rings around the neck, often making it some five times the length of the average woman's neck.

A NECKING PARTY FROM PADAUNG, Burmah. with a neck 21 inches long.

Above, AS FEATURED in Ripley's 2017 *Shatter Your Senses!*, Brittany Walsh can shoot an arrow from a bow—with her feet! As a "well-balanced" performer, she incorporates elements of contortion, balance, and danger into her stunts.

the
MAN

the
COLLECTION

the
▸ TRAVELS

the
CARTOONS

the
MEDIA

the
LOCATIONS

the
COMPANY

Modern-Day Marco Polo

Soon after his return stateside in 1923, Ripley's job at the *Globe* came to an abrupt end when the paper was shuttered. Divorced and no longer steadily employed, Ripley set sail for his *Ramble 'Round South America* in early 1925, sponsored by Associated Newspapers.

RIPLEY with a giant cigar in Rio De Janeiro, Brazil.

THE INSTITUTE is still operational today and sees more than 300,000 visitors annually.

This page, **IN SÃO PAULO**, Brazil, Ripley visited the Instituto Butantã, a biomedical research center famous for its development of antivenom, vaccines, and other medicines.

The travel installments delighted his North American readers, most of whom knew next to nothing about their "sister continent," as Ripley called it. It was this trip that would introduce him to the shrunken heads of the Shuar tribe that would become a *Believe It or Not!* icon. He purchased one for "a little less than a hundred dollars from a bootlegger of human heads in Panama City."

Dear Dug:
Best Regards to you
& Ethel ...... from
the Rio Tigre.

Rip
Buenos Aires
12 de Febrero, 1925

A POSTCARD to his brother and sister.

Above, **RIPLEY'S** sketch of his first shrunken head, which he described as "about the size of a baseball," with hair "19 inches long."

The Great Call of China

When asked what his favorite country was to visit, Robert Ripley would almost always answer with "China." From the Chinatown of his childhood in Santa Rosa, to the war-ravaged country of the 1940s, China beckoned Ripley like a siren song.

"Some of the most wonderful things in the world will seem dull and drab unless you view them in the proper light."

—Robert Ripley

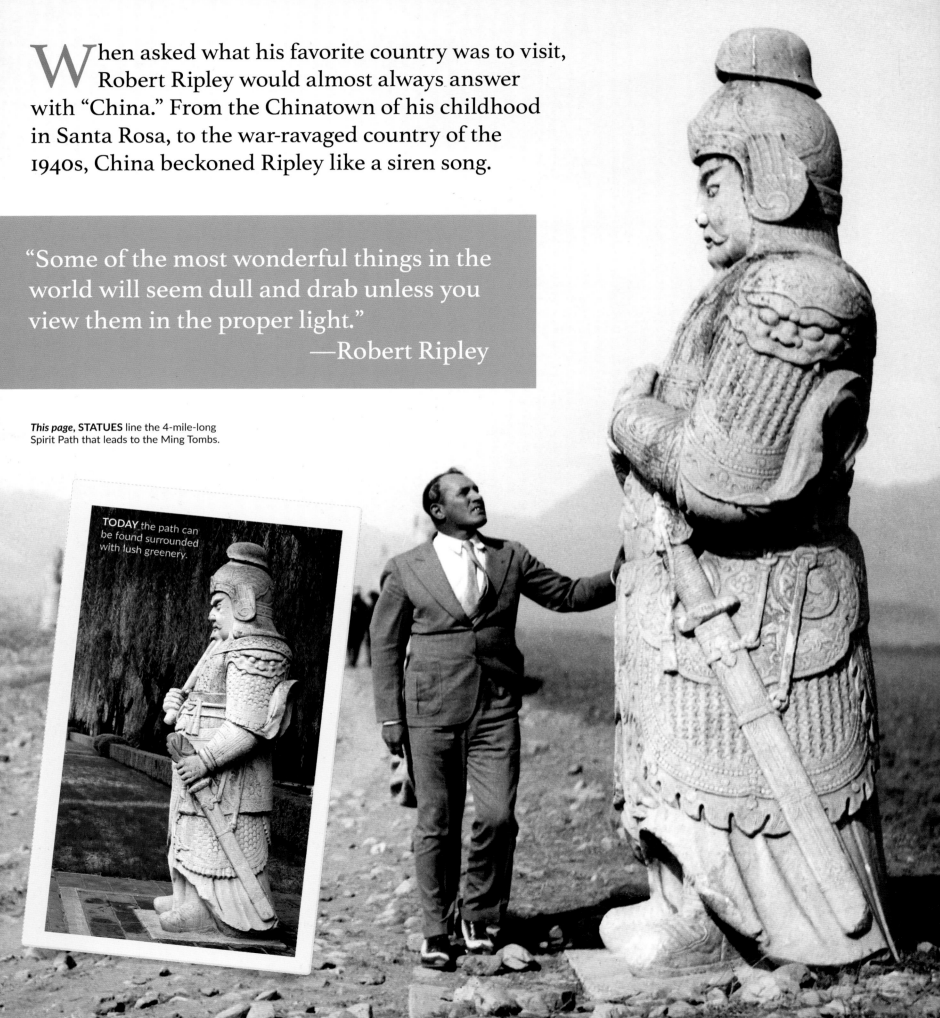

This page, **STATUES** line the 4-mile-long Spirit Path that leads to the Ming Tombs.

TODAY the path can be found surrounded with lush greenery.

THE SAME elephant pictured with Ripley below. Note the repair made to the elephant on the right.

STONING THE STONE ELEPHANT (Ming Tombs-Nanking)
CHINESE WOMEN BELIEVE THAT IF A STONE STAYS ON TOP THEY WILL HAVE A CHILD.

He preferred to stray off the beaten path, beyond tourist traps and into cities like Canton, also known as Guangzhou, which he considered the real China. Over the course of his travels throughout the years, he watched as the influence of war transformed his peaceful trips into tense, stressful journeys. Nevertheless, he continued to go and bring back stories to tell, as well as souvenirs to fill his home.

This page, CHINA'S rich history fascinated Ripley. The Ming tombs were built between 1409 and 1644.

Below, **ONE** of Ripley's favorite robes from China.

RIPLEY stands amongst what was left of Chapei, Shanghai, which had been ravaged by Japanese bombers months before his arrival.

THE IMPERIAL VAULT of Heaven, part of the Temple of Heaven, Beijing, China.

The STONE THAT SPEAKS IN THE TEMPLE of HEAVEN, PEIPING, China.
IF YOU STAND ON THIS STONE IN THE TEMPLE GROUNDS YOUR VOICE WILL BE ECHOED LOUDLY FROM BENEATH YOUR FEET
– Drawn in Peiping, 1932

RIPLEY in front of the Hall of Prayer for Good Harvests at the Temple of Heaven.

This page, **RIPLEY** with a guide pointing to an "Echo Stone" at the Temple of Heaven, Beijing, China. When a person stands upon this brick, their voice is loudly echoed back to them.

From Cairo to Cape Town

Somewhat bored by Europe and hoping to find more shock-inducing places like China and India, Ripley booked a sea and air tour of Africa, from Cairo to Cape Town.

He visited Kenya, Zanzibar, Sudan, Uganda, Tanzania, Zimbabwe (then Rhodesia), Morocco, Mozambique, and others. He fell in love with the massive continent, but at times was dismayed to see the effects of colonialism.

Below, **RIPLEY** standing at the feet of one of the Colossi of Memnon statues in Egypt.

RIPLEY in Tanzania with a victim of elephantiasis.

"I have traveled in 201 countries and the strangest thing I saw was man."
—Robert Ripley

RIPLEY interacting with schoolchildren in Omderman, Sudan.

EXTREME body modifications, like this man's stretched earlobes, continue to be a Believe It or Not! mainstay.

FILMING at Victoria Falls, which straddles both Zambia and Zimbabwe.

This page, **RIPLEY** waves while sitting on a rock below Victoria Falls, Zambia.

A TERMITE mound in Kenya towers high above Ripley.

Searching for Eden

Ripley visited a number of ancient and holy sites as he toured through Western Asia, Southern Asia, and the Middle East in countries including Iraq, Israel, Afghanistan, Jordan, Pakistan, Syria, and more.

A TOPLESS Ripley in the Garden of Eden in Iraq.

RIPLEY laughing with a group of locals in Afghanistan.

OUTSIDE THE WALLS of JERUSALEM. Sept. 28, 1933

" BELIEVE IT or NOT

PRESENT day view of what were the giant Buddhas in Bamiyan, Afghanistan.

This page, **RIPLEY** in front of one of the giant Buddhas in Bamiyan, Afghanistan, which were destroyed by the Taliban in 2001.

"The strangest places on Earth are the holiest."

—Robert Ripley

Hell & Back

Ripley's ventures throughout Europe were seemingly tame compared to his romps through Asia. But what he may have lacked in oddities, he made up for in company—for this is where Ripley met Oakie for the first time.

RIPLEY found great joy in being able to say he had been to Hell (a small town in Norway).

RIPLEY standing in front of the Palazzo Ducale and Rialto Bridge in Italy in 1925.

RIPLEY in front of the Leaning Tower of Pisa in Italy in 1931.

Above, RIPLEY with his collection of beer steins from Germany.

This page, RIPLEY standing in front of Stonehenge in 1931.

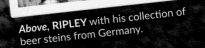

South Pacific Cruise

In 1932, Ripley found himself on the other side of the world, exploring the South Pacific on a cruise, partially in order to escape a highly publicized lawsuit against one of his scorned lovers.

In addition to a radio crew and cameraman, Ripley was joined by Ruth "Oakie" Ross aboard the *SS Mariposa.* Together over the course of three months they visited over a dozen countries, including Fiji, Australia, Papua New Guinea, Singapore, Thailand, and Japan, performing transoceanic radio broadcasts along the way.

Below, **DANCING** remains an important part of Balinese culture and typically falls within three categories: sacred (Wali), semi-sacred (Bebali), and entertainment (Balih-balihan).

This page, **RIPLEY** standing with two Balinese dancers. He considered the people of Bali to be "the most artistic on Earth."

TEMPLE OF BROKEN DISHES
THE WAT ARUN — 242 FEET HIGH
BANGKOK, SIAM
A MAGNIFICENT AND COLORFUL TEMPLE BUILT OF BROKEN DISHES SALVAGED FROM A WRECKED SHIP

Above and left, **WAT ARUN,** or the Temple of Dawn, in Bangkok, Thailand. The Buddhist structure is decorated with thousands of pieces of broken ceramic and porcelain dishes from Europe and China.

Below, **THE TEMPLE** was recently restored, resulting in a vibrant white exterior that caused controversy among those who feel the cleaning took away from the temple's charm and history.

THE TEMPLE can be found on the Thonburi west bank of the Chao Phraya River.

Ripley's EST. 1918

THE NAME *Waitomo* comes from the Māori words for water (*wai*) and sinkhole (*tomo*).

THE **CAVE** of the **GlowWorms!**

AN UNDERGROUND *FAIRYLAND* — LIGHTED BY MILLIONS OF GLOWWORMS!

(A NATURAL WONDER OF THE WORLD.)

Waitomo, N.Z.

Above and left, **THE WAITOMO** Glowworm Caves of New Zealand remain a popular tourist attraction to this day.

Below and right, **THIS PARTICULAR** sundial no longer exists and was technically never the largest sundial in the world—just the largest *university* sundial. The largest in the world is Jantar Mantar, built in India in 1728.

THE LARGEST SUNDIAL IN THE WORLD
A STRUCTURE 65 FEET LONG AND 25 FEET HIGH
—University of the Philippines, Manila

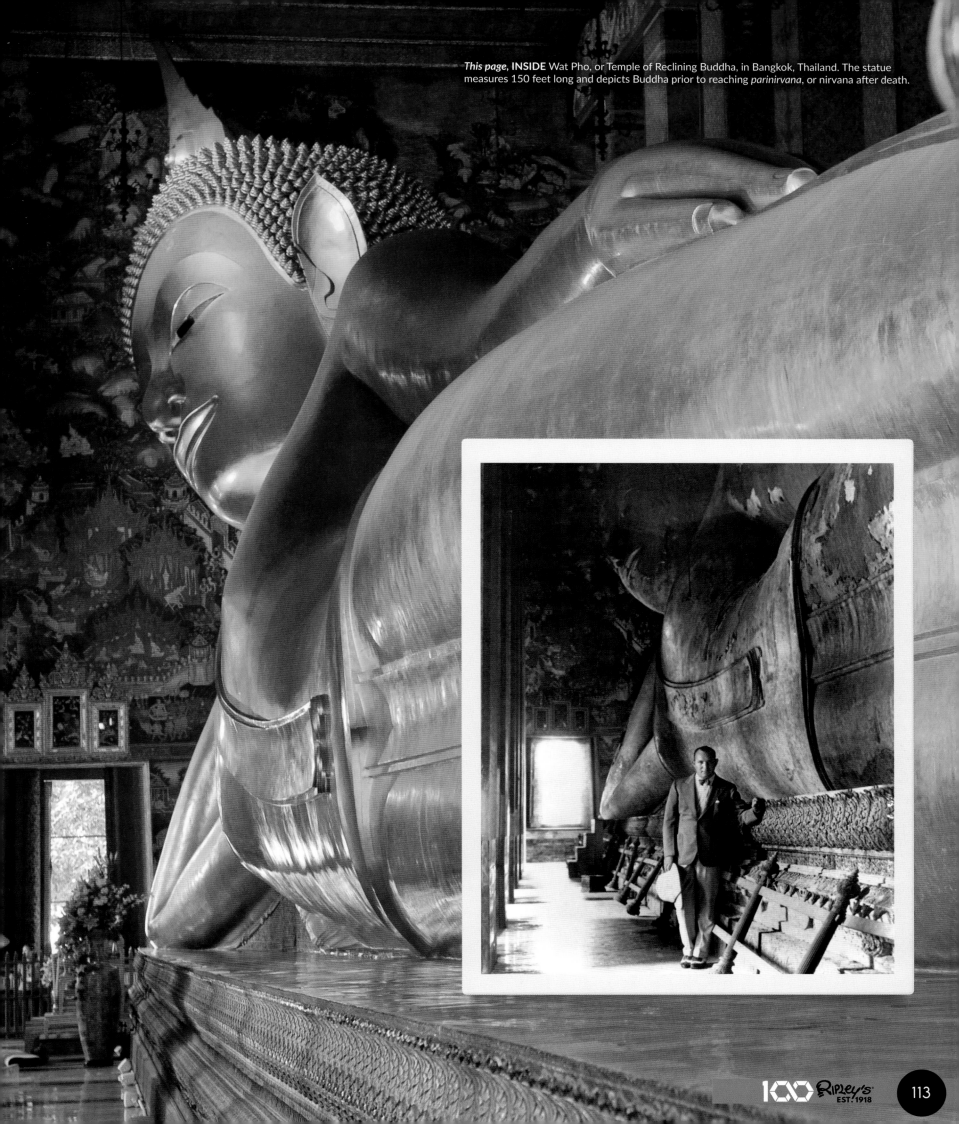

This page, **INSIDE** Wat Pho, or Temple of Reclining Buddha, in Bangkok, Thailand. The statue measures 150 feet long and depicts Buddha prior to reaching *parinirvana*, or nirvana after death.

Squalor & Splendor

Simultaneously enamored with and repulsed by the squalor in the streets, Ripley found India to be a treasure trove of "Believe It or Not!" stories. He observed ceremonial cremations along the River Ganges, gawked at the fakirs' extreme displays of religious devotion, and retraced the steps of Buddha at Bodh Gaya.

No place in the world surprised and bewildered Ripley like India. The city of Benares, also known as Varanasi, topped Ripley's list of Most Wonderful Cities in the World.

ONE of several "up arm" men Ripley came across.

AN EXTREME case of leprosy. A common sight for Ripley in India.

A FAKIR who devoted himself to the monkey god.

RIPLEY at Bodh Gaya.

This page, **RIPLEY** visited the holy Ghats along the River Ganges three days in a row during his first trip to India.

"I have traveled 20,000 miles and have seen no place which baffles description as this."
— Robert Ripley

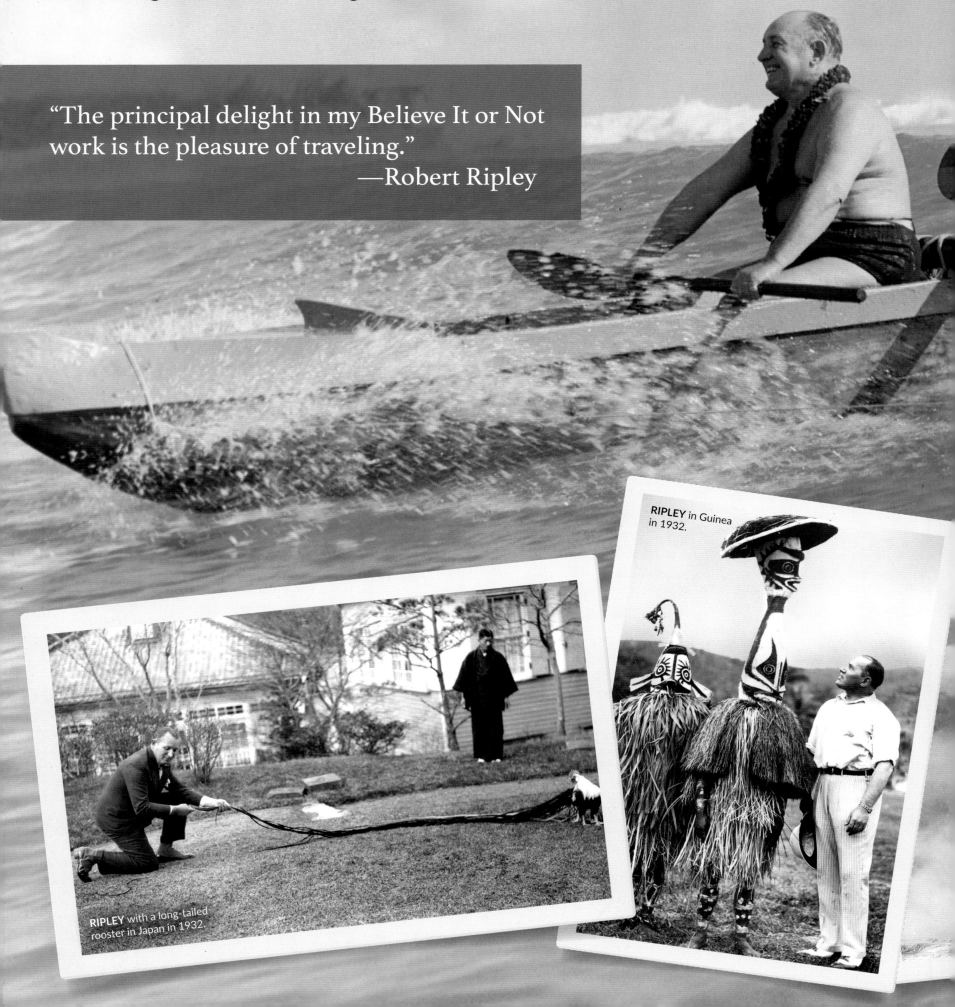

All in all, Ripley visited over 200 countries and territories, although some of those have changed names or no longer exist.

"The principal delight in my Believe It or Not work is the pleasure of traveling."
—Robert Ripley

RIPLEY in Guinea in 1932.

RIPLEY with a long-tailed rooster in Japan in 1932.

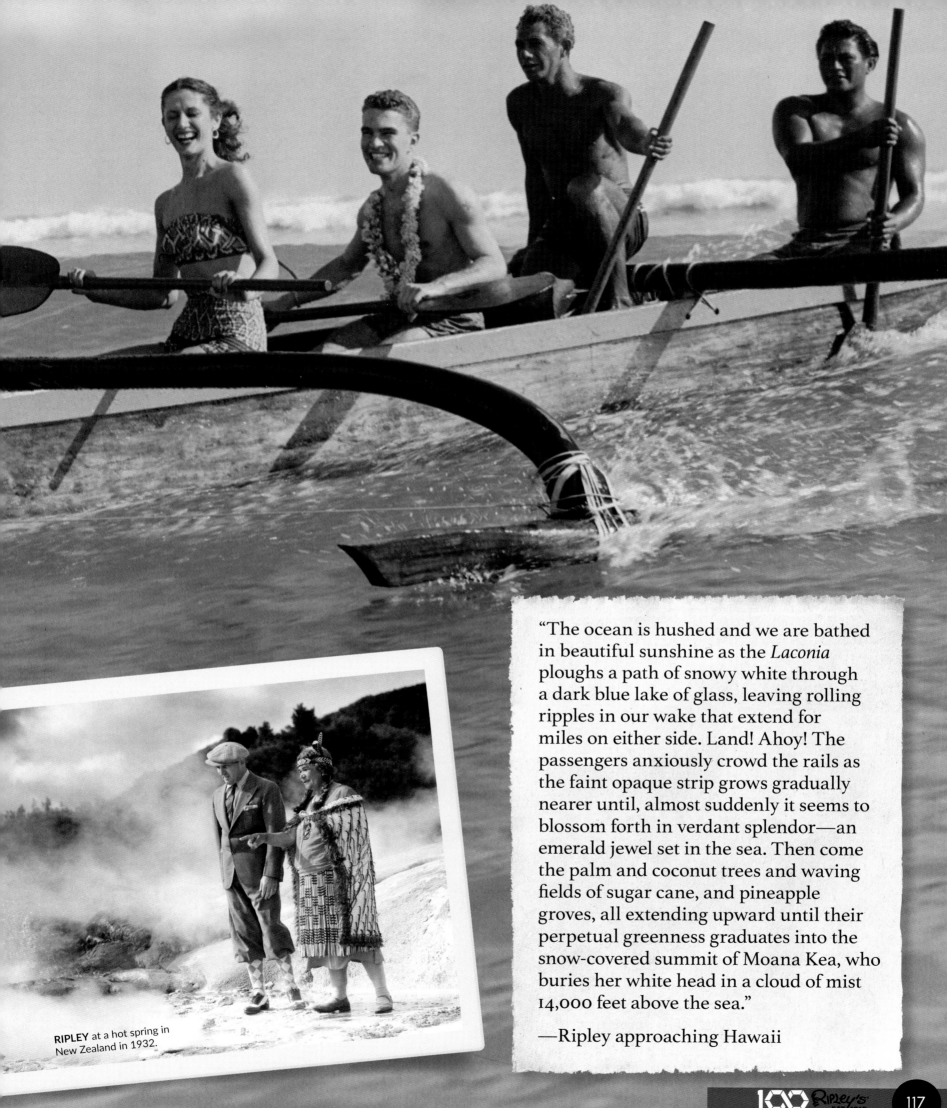

RIPLEY at a hot spring in New Zealand in 1932.

"The ocean is hushed and we are bathed in beautiful sunshine as the *Laconia* ploughs a path of snowy white through a dark blue lake of glass, leaving rolling ripples in our wake that extend for miles on either side. Land! Ahoy! The passengers anxiously crowd the rails as the faint opaque strip grows gradually nearer until, almost suddenly it seems to blossom forth in verdant splendor—an emerald jewel set in the sea. Then come the palm and coconut trees and waving fields of sugar cane, and pineapple groves, all extending upward until their perpetual greenness graduates into the snow-covered summit of Moana Kea, who buries her white head in a cloud of mist 14,000 feet above the sea."

—Ripley approaching Hawaii

The Cartoons

Foreword by John Graziano

Most kids don't know what they want to do when they grow up. I knew I had an aptitude for art, but it wasn't until a stop at the Ripley's BION Odditorium in St. Augustine, Florida, that I was propelled on a path of discovery.

There I learned of Robert Ripley and how he made a living by presenting weird and strange unbelievable facts in cartoon form. I was hooked. "THAT'S what I want to do," I said.

I researched a couple of odd facts, rendered them in pen and ink, and then dutifully sent them off to the Ripley's Believe It or Not! King Features editorial office in New York. I was 15 at the time. They wrote me back saying they liked what they had seen and forwarded the material to their corporate headquarters in Toronto.

The Canadian reply was more rooted in reality. It was obvious to them that the drawing was from a kid, but they had words of encouragement for me, saying that my work "shows promise" and to continue my education to become a professional. (They also sent me a pass to go to any of the museums for free.) Instead of crushing my dreams, their letter did the opposite.

I took that advice seriously and majored in Illustration at the Newark School of Fine and Industrial Art in New Jersey. After graduation, I worked at a T-shirt business doing illustrations for 11 years before contacting Ripley's again. I called Bob Whiteman (originally hired by Robert Ripley himself, Bob had been the sole licensing agent for Ripley's since the late '40s), and I told him about this licensing idea I had that involved drawing. He said, "Well, you know, we're looking for a cartoonist to do the strip. Why don't you send me some material?"

So I put some samples in a priority envelope, sent it out, and he called me the very next day. He goes, "John, I want you to come out here to Rye, New York, and we can talk about it." What a white-knuckle experience driving over there from New Jersey!

The rest is history. I've been rendering the feature for the past 14 years—the very first cartoon I drew for Ripley's was a Sunday released on June 27, 2004. Of course, the very first cartoon was drawn by Ripley himself in 1918, and it's the longest running syndicated cartoon in history.

Our cartoon is unique since there are no recurring characters. It's not like other strips that are driven by the love for the characters and the stories. What's kept the cartoon fresh over the years—and it still does to this day—is the "What did you see in the world today that knocked your socks off?"

I think it's been around so long because in today's era of reality TV and instant gratification, Ripley's strip was like that from the beginning. Not only did he go out and beat the bushes himself, which was harder back then with no Internet, but he also encouraged and relied on stringers, the public, and the fans to send in material.

The cartoon has gone through a few changes, though. Today you can see it online and subscribe to the Ripley's strip for free. People can leave comments on the web page instead of writing in, and just like in Ripley's time, there's still a lot of controversy when you put a "believe it or not" out there. The cartoon makes people happy or angry, and you get a sense of that right away from reading the comments section.

Over the years, there have been six cartoonists who have drawn the strip. Out of all the previous artists that have done the Ripley cartoon, I love the work of Paul Frehm (he was the second cartoonist).

The Cartoons

Don't get me wrong, Ripley was a great artist, but Frehm had a totally different style. I learn a lot from looking at his artwork, because it's so researched and it's got an accuracy to it. He's the only one who won the National Cartoonists Division Award in the category of Newspaper Panel in 1976 for his work on the *Ripley's Believe It or Not!* panel. There's something to be said for that.

In Ripley and Frehm's time, the syndicate, which was King Features then, would only sell to newspapers. Now United Media, our current syndicate, actively tries to get us in other markets. When we switched syndicates in 1989, we were added to GoComics.com, which has about 550 strips, including classics like *Dick Tracy.*

The syndicate also does colorization, which is a major thing because, traditionally, the dailies have only been black and white. The only color has been Sundays. If certain magazines or newspapers wanted the dailies in color, they would have to color it themselves, which is how we have some older cartoons in color. They weren't done by King Features; they were done by the newspaper or the magazine. United Media picked up coloring dailies around 2007 to be more competitive with daily newspapers that had color sections.

Content-wise, for a while we were bringing back more puzzles and two-parters, which Ripley loved to do, but as we became more global, the two-parters didn't work as well (not all the papers and syndicates would have the dailies and the Sunday). We also used to feature certain holidays, but that became too America-centric, and we want the strip to appeal to everyone, so we keep it more global.

It's becoming more of a challenge to get more unbelievable material for the strip, but sometimes you have to look to history. Ripley's long-term researcher, Norbert Pearlroth, spent most of his time in the New York Public Library. He was searching newspapers, yes, but he was also going back and looking at history to find unbelievable facts. We still do that today.

The Internet makes it tougher for us because most people see weird news all the time. To differentiate ourselves and pick up on some less publicized but equally unbelievable stories, we still go back to our grass roots, with people submitting on a local level.

I truly have a passion for what I do. To me, it's not a job. Ripley said it himself: when you get up in the morning and you're doing what you love to do, you feel like you're not working. And that's how it is, and that's how it's been.

I sincerely hope I am doing him proud.

Thanks, "Rip."

All the Best!
from Ripley

"Believe It or Not" Ripley

Believe It
— or Not

Above, **RIPLEY** hard at work at his drawing board, circa late 1940s.

Left, **JOHN GRAZIANO** hard at work at his drawing board, 2018.

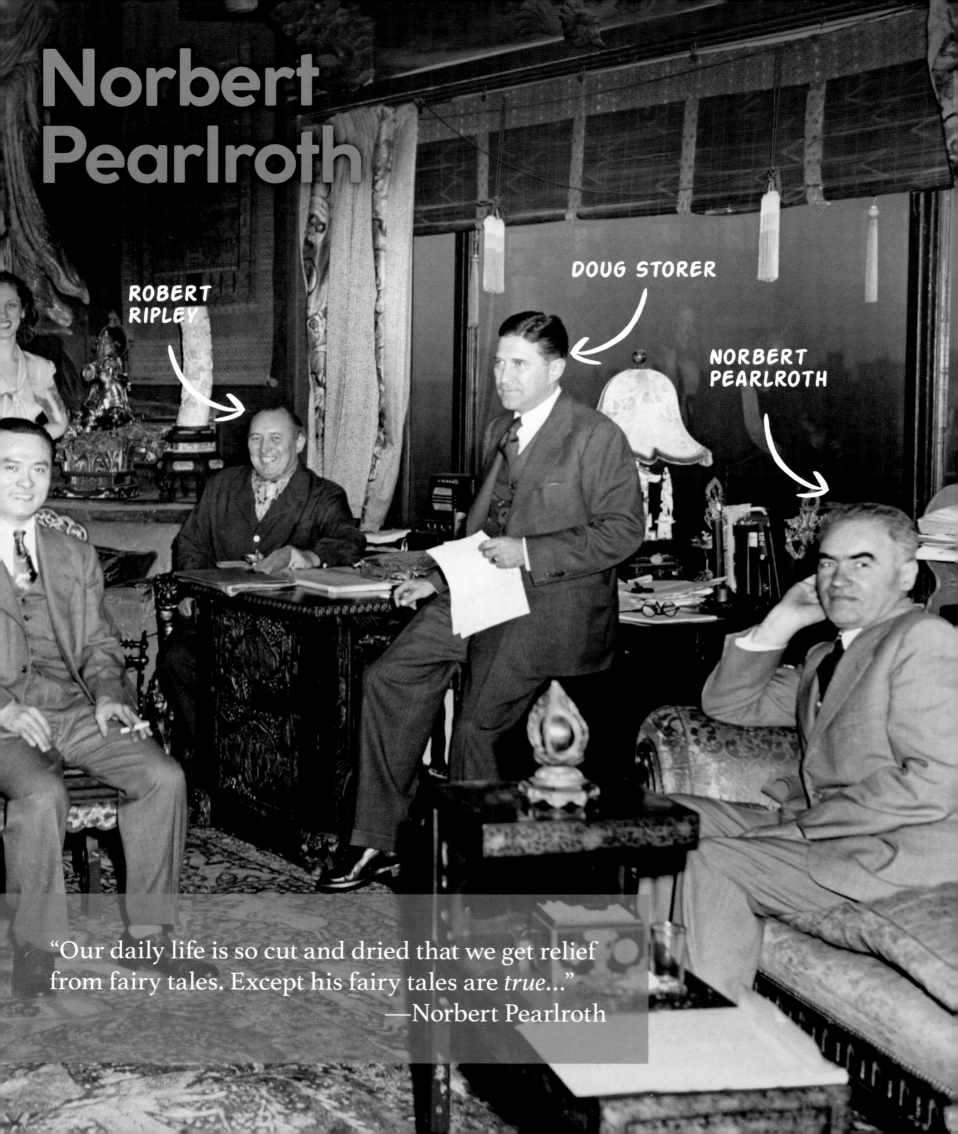

Norbert Pearlroth

ROBERT RIPLEY

DOUG STORER

NORBERT PEARLROTH

"Our daily life is so cut and dried that we get relief from fairy tales. Except his fairy tales are *true*..."
—Norbert Pearlroth

PEARLROTH

How did a bookish bank worker become the driving force behind the man?

In 1923, Ripley was looking for a linguist and translator when Norbert Pearlroth, fluent in about a dozen languages, showed up for an interview and scored the job, initially just an hour-a-week commitment.

But when the *Believe It or Not!* cartoons gained momentum, Pearlroth quit his bank job to work full-time gathering unique facts, taking Ripley's handwritten ideas and schoolboy notebooks to new heights.

Preferring to spend each day locked in the New York Public Library on Fifth Avenue rather than being in the limelight, he was the perfect partner for the eccentric Ripley.

Pearlroth eventually helped Ripley make the most of his worldly travels, preparing itineraries for him. "You can't just take off for a country and ask the natives where their curiosities are. You have to come primed, you have to already know about them," he once lectured Ripley.

Ripley's bookworm

He dug up facts stranger than fiction, believe it or not

Norbert Pearlroth, 52 years a researcher for Ripley and King Features Syndicate, holds a volume of illustrations for which he provided the facts

Lindbergh Cartoon

Taking his talents to the *New York Evening Post* in 1926, Ripley soon delivered his most contentious "Believe It or Not" yet.

"Rip's" Most Doubted "Believe It or Not"

LINDBERGH WAS THE 67th MAN TO MAKE A NON-STOP FLIGHT OVER THE ATLANTIC OCEAN!

***Above,* THE CARTOON** appeared after Lindbergh's famous flight in 1927, claiming that he was not the first man to successfully fly across the Atlantic; he was actually the 67th.

In May 1927, Charles Lindbergh successfully completed his nonstop solo flight across the Atlantic, prompting a media frenzy. And then Ripley published a cartoon that would incite the masses.

By omitting the word "solo," Ripley printed a recklessly true fact. Readers, however, angrily responded to his claim, with Ripley receiving phone calls, telegrams, and thousands of complaint letters within a matter of days.

But he didn't stop there. "Buffalo Bill never shot a buffalo in his life. . .George Washington was not the first president of the United States"—Ripley created more cartoons designed to engage and enrage the public. He didn't mind being called a liar; in fact, he loved it.

"It makes no difference what I say, you won't believe me anyway."
—Robert Ripley

This page, **LINDBERGH** with the plane he flew across the Atlantic, *Spirit of St. Louis.*

Making American History

O n November 3, 1929—just a week after the stock
market crash—Ripley made a shameless
statement in his first Sunday panel for Randolph
Hearst: "America Has No National Anthem."

The sensitive, writhing public went catatonic as Ripley correctly asserted
that "The Star-Spangled Banner" was nothing more than an unofficial
anthem, with the melody lifted from an old English drinking song.

But it took a little more than a year for Congress to pass a one-
sentence bill, and on March 3, 1931, President Herbert Hoover signed
into law "The Star-Spangled Banner" as America's national anthem—all
thanks to Mr. Ripley.

PRESIDENT Herbert Hoover signed Public Law
823 declaring "The Star-Spangled Banner" the
national anthem.

Below, **THE CARTOON** appeared on the November 3, 1929, Sunday panel, originally in black and white.

It was Ripley who helped to make "The Star-Spangled Banner" the official United States anthem. Congress had repeatedly refused to recognize it as such.

On November 3, 1929, a Believe it or Not cartoon was published with this caption: AMERICA HAS NO NATIONAL ANTHEM. The United States—being a dry country—has been using without authorization—an old English drinking song ("To Anacreon in Heaven").

As a result of this cartoon more than 5 million petitions descended upon Congress. There were letters from people in all walks of life. Invariably they referred in shocked accents to the Believe it or Not cartoon. "Can this be true?"—they queried—"and why isn't something done about it?" Something was done. On March 3, 1931, Congress finally passed a resolution making "The Star-Spangled Banner" the official United States anthem.

I Dare You to Prove Me Wrong

At the height of his popularity, Ripley's cartoons were published in more than 360 newspapers around the world, translated into 17 languages, with a daily readership of 80 million people. The haters abounded.

Ripley was constantly inundated with letters complaining and demanding proof to verify his unbelievable claims.

One man took it upon himself to personally prove Ripley wrong. Wayne Harbour from Bedford, Iowa, spent 29 years writing letters to various authorities seeking verification for hundreds of cartoons (even occasionally submitting a few toons that Ripley featured). Believe it or not, in nearly three decades of searching, Harbour never once received a reply contradicting a Ripley cartoon fact.

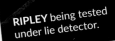

RIPLEY being tested under lie detector.

This page, **RIPLEY** on Trial. For one of his Vitaphone movies, Ripley staged a mock trial where he took the stand while a judge presided over the interrogation, a district attorney grilling him on the unbelievable stories detailed in his book.

Below, **HARBOUR** kept all the answers he received in scrapbooks, which he donated to Ripley Entertainment. At last count, he had sent 24,241 letters of inquiry and received 11,115 replies. His unbelievable self-imposed mission was the subject of a couple cartoons, the last being in 1962, 10 years before he would stop verifying *Ripley's Believe It or Not!* cartoons.

Ripley's —— **Believe It or Not!**

WAYNE HARBOUR of Bedford, Iowa, AS A HOBBY HAS WRITTEN A LETTER TO CONFIRM THE AUTHENTICITY OF EVERY ITEM IN **BELIEVE IT OR NOT** DURING THE PAST 19 YEARS!

HE HAS WRITTEN 17,172 LETTERS, SPENT NEARLY $1,500 IN POSTAGE, DEVOTED 7,167 HOURS TO HIS HOBBY— AND FILLED 75 SCRAPBOOKS WITH REPLIES FROM EVERY CORNER OF THE WORLD

Oldest Man Who Ever Lived

In one of his most disputed cartoons, Ripley asserted that Li Yung of China was the oldest man who had ever lived.

The dubious cartoon panel appeared on January 16, 1944, immediately causing thousands of letters demanding proof to flood Ripley's office.

Contests

King Features launched a series of contests offering various prizes to readers with the best strange-but-true stories and items. Successful local contests gave way to the first national *Believe It or Not* contest in 1932—with 2.5 million letters in just two weeks!

There were three more national contests, the last taking place in 1945. With so many new stories and facts, Ripley was never at a loss for cartoon fodder.

Editors: Start the Contest off fast by publishing this ad April 28

HOW WOULD YOU
like your choice of these prizes?

Curtiss-Wright Monoplane, with complete course at flying school

Trip through Province of Quebec, two weeks, for two people, all expenses

Trip to Havana via Ward Line two weeks, for two people, all expenses, with week at National Hotel

RCA Victor Radio-Phonograph with Home Recording

Wm. A. Rogers Ltd. Silver Cabinet, 87 pieces

Rockne Six "65" deluxe Sedan

Jenkins Radiovisor television set

The New Encyclopaedia Britannica— 24 volumes

Gruen Guild Curvé Watch

ROBERT L. RIPLEY, famous creator of "Believe It or Not", wants to find the world's most interesting oddities. And in return, the men, women, boys and girls who submit the best "Believe It or Nots" in the National Ripley "Believe It or Not" Contest will be allowed their choice of these Grand Prizes! Like a lot of Ripley facts, it sounds too good to be true, but it is!

The contest involves no work—no essays, no puzzles to solve, no drawings, no fancy work. Just write out your "Believe It or Not" with proof that it's true, and send it in to this paper. Send one, two, ten, a dozen—as many as you like. They all will be eligible for the contest!

Ripley has proved that we live in a world surrounded by "Believe It or Nots". One of his most famous was a fact everyone knew but didn't think of: "Lindbergh was the 67th man to make a non-stop flight across the Atlantic." Alcock and Brown and two Zeppelins carrying 64 passengers made the flight before him! Again, seven million persons live on the banks of the East River in New York City, yet they were astounded when Ripley told them: "The East River has a mouth at both ends and flows in both directions!"

See how many "Believe It or Not" facts you can unearth. You'll be surprised how easy it is to find them. Some familiar fact in your work, your home, your school, your hobby may be the "Believe It or Not" that will astound the country—and entitle you to carry off a Grand Prize.

The National
RIPLEY **BELIEVE IT OR NOT** CONTEST
May 3 to 16

SPECIAL! See the list of daily prizes on Page 00...and read the daily contest stories for further suggestions EVERY DAY in

NAME YOUR PAPER

RIPLEY rummaging through letters and submissions in his attic.

ONLY TWO MORE DAYS TO WIN $1000.00

Best Believe It or Not About the War

...AROLD ...KHURST ...ELF AND LIT A CIGARETTE ...S UPSIDEDOWN IN MIDAIR ...LTITUDE OF 20,000 FEET! ...15000 FEET BEFORE ...ENING HIS CHUTE

...you must send your Believe ...Not to Robert L. Ripley today ...morrow to win the $1000 he ...t pay for the best Believe It or ...t about the war. If you have ...ready sent in one or more, you ...an submit others, provided your ...letter is postmarked before mid-night, February 3.

You have nothing to buy. Literary merit doesn't count. Your Believe It or Not doesn't have to be a personal experience. The only requirement is that it be true and provable. The incident pictured is an example of a Believe It or Not chosen by Ripley. Do you know a better one? See the few, simple rules in page 00, and send in yours today for $1000 in cash may be awaiting you.

THESE ARE THE ONLY RULES

ANYONE CAN WIN IT $1000.00 CASH

YES, ONE THOUSAND DOLLARS WILL BE PAID THE NEWSPAPER READER SENDING R. L. RIPLEY THE BEST BELIEVE IT OR NOT ABOUT THE WAR

...U DON'T HAVE TO BE IN ...SERVICE TO COMPETE

CORPORAL LEONARD KOWALSKY BRONX, N.Y. LOST HIS CIGARETTE LIGHTER IN NEW YORK IN 1941—AND FOUND IT AGAIN IN 1944—IN ITALY— WHEN A BUDDY OFFERED HIM A LIGHT!

ANY person may compete. You need not be a service man or woman. Your Believe It or Not about the war does not have to be a personal experience. The only stipulation is that it must be TRUE and provable. Every statement submitted will receive Ripley's personal attention and he will be the sole judge.

Can You Write a 'Believe It or Not' Fact?

Every man, woman and child, regardless of age or where they live, can take part in The Herald and Examiner's new Ripley "Believe It or Not" contest. It costs absolutely nothing to enter, and all you have to do is to submit an unusual or unbelievable fact. Thirty-two daily and seven grand prizes will be awarded to the winners. Complete details of this interesting and fascinating contest will be found on Page 15 of this edition.

LAST DAY TO WIN $1000.00

For the Best Believe It or Not About the War

All entries in the contest for the best Believe It or Not about the war being conducted by Robert L. Ripley in co-operation with this newspaper, must be mailed TODAY. None postmarked after midnight, February 3, can be considered under the rules of the contest.

The few simple rules are published today beside Ripley's Believe It or Not feature. Read them and send in a Believe It or Not about the war. It can win a $1000 prize.

The prizewinner will be announced as soon ... judging is completed.

All Entries Must Be Addressed to Robert L. Ripley, care of

NAME OF PAPER

YOU MAY DISCOVER A HERO

SERGEANT MAJOR WILLIAM YASI U.S.M.C. HAS SERVED 30 YEARS IN THE MARINE CORPS. WITH NO TIME LOST!

WIN $1000

For the Best Believe It or Not About the War

Some extraordinary facts and examples of courage, devotion and achievement are coming to public notice for the first time through Robert L. Ripley's Believe It or Not feature. From personal observation, possibly through a letter from the front, or perhaps as a result of research, you may also have discovered one—and the one that will win the $1000 prize for the best Believe It or Not about the war—Read the rules below and send it in.

THESE ARE THE ONLY RULES

YOU CAN WIN $1000.00

SEND IN A "BELIEVE IT OR NOT" ABOUT THE WAR TO ROBERT L. RIPLEY TODAY

ADMIRALTY ISLANDS - SOUTH PACIFIC ...VT. DAMON SMITH – Junction City, Ore ...UDDENLY CAME FACE-TO-FACE WITH A JAP. ...OTH GRABBED FOR THEIR RIFLE AND FIRED! ...HE FIRST BULLET FROM SMITH'S GUN ...CORED A PERFECT HIT IN THE MUZZLE ...OF THE JAP'S RIFLE SEALING IT!

Airplane Trips Among Prizes in Ripley Contest

TWO round trips to New Orleans by American ...und trips

HAPPY LANDING!

IN 1938 A PLANE MADE A FORCED LANDING IN A CORNFIELD, IN GEORGETOWN, MISS. THE FARMER'S SON, U. L. BROWN, WATCHED THE REPAIR JOB AND DECIDED TO BECOME AN AVIATOR. TODAY HE IS FLYING THE BURMA ROUTE TO CHINA AS PILOT ON THE SAME PLANE!

DO YOU KNOW A BELIEVE IT OR NOT ABOUT THE WAR MORE INTERESTING THAN THIS ONE?

YOU CAN WIN $1000

Robert L. Ripley is carrying on a great search for Believe It or Nots about the war, and will pay $1000 cash for the best one sent to him. You can win it. You do not have to be in the service to compete. It doesn't have to be a personal experience. The only qualification is that the Believe It or Not about the war you submit must be absolutely TRUE and provable. The rules are simple. Read them now, and send in your Believe It or Not about the war today—you can submit as many Believe It or Nots about the war as you wish.

HERE ARE THE ONLY RULES:

The purpose of this contest is to bring out outstanding facts or examples of cour- ...ber of different "Believe It or Nots," how- ...are devotion or unusual achievement re- ...ever, each must be submitted on a separate ...

Believe It or Not!

Have you entered your unusual or unbelievable fact the Ripley "Believe It or Not" contest? Fame and ... the winners of this interesting and fascinat-... ... ug up strange facts. Details will

---

TEASER ANNOUNCEMENTS OF THE CONTEST: RUN THEM THE WEE...

$1000.00 FOR THE BEST ...ve It-Or-Not

...n win it. The Believe It or Not ...n doesn't have to be a ...experience. It can be the ...search, for example. Here ...It or Not about the war ...ipley. If you know a bet-...can win the $1000 prize.

B. I. O. N.

Means Believe It or Not. It can also mean $1000 to you. Yes, $1000.00

Ripley will pay that sum in cash for a Believe It or Not about the war. Below is an example of a Believe It or Not about the war chosen by Ripley. Do you know a better one?

Corporal GLORIA LYNCH ...YOUNGEST AIR PATROL PARACHUTIST ...WEIGHS 90 POUNDS HER CHUTE WEIGHS 60 POUNDS

Every family has a Believe It or Not about the war. Yours may bring $1000.00

Robert L. Ripley will pay $1000 in cash for a Believe It or Not about the war. Below is an example of a war Believe It or Not chosen by Ripley. Do you know a better one?

A MARINE ON GUADAL-CANAL DISCOVERED HIS BROTHER'S IDENTIFICATION TAG ON A DEAD JAP.

JULES SOUZA New Bedford, Mass. WEARS A BLACK TIE WHICH HIS BROTHER WORE IN MOURNING FOR HIM AFTER HE WAS REPORTED DEAD. HE WAS RESCUED AFTER 32 DAYS OF STARVATION ON A RAFT.

YOU CAN WIN $1000

...WILLIAMS ...OF THE ARMY

After sifting through millions of submissions, the 1932 first-prize winner was announced. Clinton Blume won a monoplane with a complete course at a flying school.

RIPLEY shaking hands with 1932 grand prize winner Clinton Blume.

BELIEVE IT OR NOT—By RI.
(Copyright, 1932)

CLINTON W. BLUME
1400 Ocean Parkway, Brooklyn
LOST A SCRUB BRUSH AT SEA, WHEN
ARMY TRANSPORT SANK 500 MILES OFF COAST OF FRANCE,
AND IT WAS WASHED ASHORE AT HIS FEET IN BROOKLYN
ONE YEAR LATER!
6-20-32

TOWERS ABOVE THEM *ALL*

Believe It or Not!
by *Ripley*

THE great promotion plan described in the accompanying pages and supplied free to newspapers using *BELIEVE IT OR NOT* is just another reason why your newspaper should have this peerless feature.

Analysis of the *Continuing Studies of Newspaper Reading* conducted by the Advertising Research Foundation of the ANA and AAAA in co-operation with the ANPA, shows that Ripley's *BELIEVE IT OR NOT* tops every other feature in reader interest, with the single exception of front page news pictures.

More newspapers publish Ripley's *BELIEVE IT OR NOT* today than before the war, and Ripley's *BELIEVE IT OR NOTs* about the war have made it more interesting than ever.

Any editor in whose territory *BELIEVE IT OR NOT* is available should have it. There is no substitute. There is only one *BELIEVE IT OR NOT.*

Supplied daily in two and three columns; Sunday in standard half page and standard third page in color, also in four column black and white.

YOU DO NOT, OF COURSE, HAVE TO USE THIS CONTEST TO GET UNEXCELLED READER ATTENTION WITH BELIEVE IT OR NOT

BUY IT NOW!

WRITE OR WIRE TODAY TO F. J. NICHT, GEN. SALES MGR.

KING
FEATURES
SYNDICATE

235 E. 45th St., New York 17

$1000.00 FOR THE BEST BELIEVE IT OR NOT ABOUT THE WAR

BIBLE SAVED HIS LIFE

Pfc. ARTHUR ANDERSON
St. Paul, Minn.

WAS CARRYING A SMALL BIBLE IN HIS BREAST POCKET WHEN HIT BY SHRAPNEL MIRACULOUSLY THE WORD ON WHICH THE MOST POWERFUL BIT OF SHRAPNEL SPENT ITS STRENGTH WAS "CLEMENCY"

THE NEW "BELIEVE IT OR NOT" NEWSPAPER CONTEST FOR YOU— A GREAT PROMOTION PLAN FOR YOUR PAPER THAT COSTS YOU NOTHING

INSURING his hold on the attention of service men and their kin, and enlarging his circulation among them, is basic in the post-war planning of every newspaper editor.

So this new Robert L. Ripley BELIEVE IT OR NOT CONTEST about the war is designed to give any newspaper a flying start now in that direction.

A BELIEVE IT OR NOT contest NEVER FAILS to get and hold interest of readers. The first national BELIEVE IT OR NOT newspaper contest in 1932, in which 153 newspapers participated, brought in over 1,500,000 entries. A second, put on in 1935 by popular demand of circulation managers, topped this total. A third contest in 1938, again by request of BELIEVE IT OR NOT clients, set another record. But here comes the biggest and best BELIEVE IT OR NOT contest of all—with a prize of $1000 in cash for the best BELIEVE IT OR NOT about the war sent in by any reader of a participating paper.

The contest undoubtedly will bring out stories of achievement and heroism in the war that would otherwise pass unnoted. Thus it will serve a useful purpose in the war effort.

ANY PERSON MAY ENTER

The contestant does not have to be a service man or woman. Any reader can compete and win.

This contest costs the participating newspaper nothing. This great promotion stunt is FREE to all newspapers using the Ripley daily or Sunday BELIEVE IT OR NOT cartoons.

Every reader whose BELIEVE IT OR NOT about the war is used by Ripley in his cartoon will receive an autographed copy of the big book of BELIEVE IT OR NOT published by Simon & Schuster and will, of course, be credited in the cartoon. The reader whose BELIEVE IT OR NOT about the war is chosen by Ripley as the best submitted during the contest will be given $1000 in cash by King Features Syndicate.

Every man in the service has a BELIEVE IT OR NOT about the war. Nearly every non-service man or woman in the country also has one—it may be based on something a service kinsman has written home or upon personal experience or research. Every person is a potential entrant in the contest. And every entrant will watch the participating newspaper for publication of his BELIEVE IT OR NOT or for contest news.

NO WORRIES ABOUT MAIL

You do NOT have to set up a contest department and handle mail. You can have all entries addressed to Ripley in care of your newspaper, and forward the letters to him in bulk; or you can have readers address him directly at his New York office. In either case, EVERY LETTER REACHING RIPLEY'S OFFICE WILL BE ACKNOWLEDGED BY MR. RIPLEY. The contestant will not be left in doubt about whether his or her letter was received.

All judging will be done by Ripley. No matter how many entries there are, the contestants are assured that Ripley himself will decide on the merits of their contributions.

ONLY SMALL SPACE REQUIRED

All promotion for this contest has been streamlined. All ads are limited to one, two and three column size—most are one column. You do not have to give up much of your precious space to get big results with this contest.

Except for news stories, all promotion matter is available to you in matted form—very little composition is necessary.

DATES OF CONTEST

The contest period is January 15 to February 3 Papers using Sunday Ripley releases should begin January 14; papers using daily releases only should start January 15

Winner will be announced as soon thereafter as judging is completed. We hope to make the announcement early in January.

WRITE OR WIRE FOR MATS TODAY

All you have to do to have your newspaper participate in this contest is:

1. Write or wire today for mats of contest promotion. (Photo prints of halftones will be supplied, upon request, if you wish to make your own engravings.) Address requests to CASWELL ADAMS, King Features Syndicate, 235 East 45th St., New York 17.

2. Start promoting the contest two or three days before it starts, and use some kind of promotion daily during the contest to insure best results. Decide whether you wish to have contest mail addressed to Ripley in care of your newspaper or directly to his New York office and make promotion conform.

3. Run the contest rules daily. (This is required by the Post Office Department.)

4. Forward all contest mail to Ripley, at 235 East 45th Street, New York 17, N. Y., *DAILY*.

SEE NEXT PAGE →

The Illustrators

In a century of *Believe It or Not!* cartoons, only six illustrators have assumed the mantle left behind by Ripley at his death, each one bringing new life to the oldest syndicated cartoon in history.

1. **Robert Ripley**—1918–1949

2. **Paul Frehm**—1949–1977

3. **Walter Frehm**—1978–1989

4. **Kelly Brine**—November–December 1989, February–March 1990

5. **Randy Timms**—December 1989–February 1990

6. **Don Wimmer**—March 1990–2004

7. **John Graziano**—2004–present day

Above, **ROBERT RIPLEY,** *Believe It or Not!* artist from 1918–1949, drawn by John Graziano.

Below, cartoon panel summarizing Ripley's life by cartoonist Jo Hochmann in 1928.

RIPLEY with other cartoonists.

ROBERT RIPLEY

Parker Quink

PAUL FREHM
sketch drawn by
John Graziano.

GRAZIANO

Paul Frehm
Ripley artist from 1949 to 1977

Above, **WITH KING FEATURES SYNDICATE**, Paul Frehm made illustrations for feature stories and trials, most importantly for the trial of Bruno Hauptmann, the kidnapper of the Lindbergh baby in 1932.

Paul Frehm was born in Brooklyn in 1904 and attended the Pratt Institute in New York. He began as a staff artist at *The New York American* and then transferred to *The Mirror*. Prior to becoming the Ripley artist, he did fill-ins for a busy Bob Ripley. After Ripley's death, Frehm became the lead cartoonist for the feature. In 1976, he was bestowed the National Cartoonists Division Award in the category of Newspaper Panel for his work on the *Ripley's Believe It or Not!* panel.

Born in 1906, Walter was Paul Frehm's younger brother. Also gaining an art education from the Pratt Institute, he worked on a couple comic strips before joining King Features Syndicate in 1958 as an editor in the comics department. He helped his brother Paul churn out the *Believe It or Not!* newspaper feature and then took over as lead cartoonist in 1978 when Paul retired.

Walter Frehm
Ripley artist from 1978 to 1989

WALTER FREHM sketch drawn by John Graziano.

Ripley's — **Believe It or Not!**

A **CHEETAH** CAN ACCELERATE FROM ZERO TO 45 MILES PER HOUR IN 2 SECONDS

WOMEN ARE THE SOLE BREADWINNERS OF 8,500,000 *AMERICAN FAMILIES* Submitted by Tom Higgins, Grahamsville, N.Y.

A MICKEY MANTLE BASEBALL CA ISSUED IN 1952 AND OWNED BY of Coram, N.Y., IS VALUE

Ripley's — **Believe It or Not!**

Ripley's — **Believe It or Not!**

THE **NATIONAL HORSE SHOW** ONE OF NEW YORK'S SOCIAL HIGH-LIGHTS-- WHEN INITIALLY STAGED IN 1883 WAS CALLED THE *FIRST ANNUAL SHOW OF HORSES, PONIES, MULES AND DONKEYS*

FOR RENT

AD WERE FOR NON-RENT EXICO'S HE 1920s Y THE AND D TO HE SESSED rights reserved.

ANNA HELD THE FAMOUS FRENCH ACTRESS HAD HER LOWER RIBS REMOVED BY A SURGEON TO REDUCE THE SIZE OF HER WAIST

KUNG FU A TERM N AMERICA TO DESCRIBE A CHINESE OF FIGHTING, IS A MISNOMER AND ACTUALLY S *"TO HAVE A SKILL" IN ANYTHING*

THE **BLACK WIDOW SPIDER** HAS A VENOMOUS BITE THAT CAN KILL A HUMAN, YET IT IS EATEN WITH IMPU-NITY BY PIGEONS, WASPS AND HENS

Ripley's — **Believe It or Not!**

MEL BLANC WHO WAS THE VOICE OF THE BUGS BUNNY CARTOON CHARACTER *WAS ALLERGIC TO CARROTS*

TOMATO SOUP

A CAN OF **TOMATO SOUP** PRODUCED IN THE U.S., IS SUBJECT TO MORE THAN **100 FEDERAL LAWS**

SELF-PORTRAIT

Don Wimmer
Ripley artist from 1990 to 2004

Don Wimmer from New Jersey graduated from Kean University with a degree in visual communications. He did freelance illustration until he started as the Ripley's artist in 1990. He drew the feature for 14 years. Today he writes and draws the newspaper family comic *Rose Is Rose*.

"I was flown up to Canada to meet with Edward Meyer and my researcher, Karen Kemlo. I could tell Ripley's was a real family and I always felt welcomed, even though I was drawing from a different country. . . I have fond memories of my time with Ripley's and made lifelong friends."

"One of my favorite adventures was going to Bryant Park in New York City to sketch the world's largest chicken pot pie."
— Don Wimmer

Ripley's — Believe It or Not!

Believe It or Not! DES ALLEMANDS, LA., IS KNOWN AS "THE CATFISH CAPITAL of the UNIVERSE"! SUBMITTED BY RICHARD GIBSON, LAFAYETTE, LA.

WOMEN IN ANCIENT ROME DYED THEIR HAIR BLONDE USING A MIXTURE of BEECHWOOD ASH and GOAT FAT! THEY ALSO USED A CONDITIONER MADE from PEPPER, DEER MARROW, BEAR GREASE and RATS' HEAD!

DURING THE 1904 OLYMPIC GAMES THERE WAS AN EVENT CALLED "THE PLUNGE for DISTANCE," IN WHICH SWIMMERS DOVE INTO A POOL AND GLIDED UNDERWATER AS FAR AS THEY COULD BEFORE BEING FORCED UP for AIR!

IN THE FIRST HOUR AFTER IT IS BORN, A NEWBORN BABY CAN IMITATE AN ADULT WHO IS STICKING OUT HIS TONGUE!

PFFFT...

GÖRAN KROPP RODE A BICYCLE 7,000 MILES from HIS HOME IN Sweden to Nepal, THEN CLIMBED THE 29,028-ft.-HIGH Mount Everest ALONE, THEN BICYCLED BACK HOME AGAIN!

© 2001 Ripley Entertainment Inc.
Dist. by United Feature Syndicate, Inc.
www.comics.com
1-14

Ripley's — Believe It or Not!

IN Paranaque City, the Philippines, A PERSON CAN WALK from BETHLEHEM to JERUSALEM and the UNITED STATES to UPPER VOLTA IN A MATTER of MINUTES! They are all street names! SUBMITTED BY DAVID MURPHY, PARANAQUE CITY, THE PHILIPPINES

A LABRADOR PUPPY OWNED BY Eliza Hastings of Gloucestershire, England, SWALLOWED HER £800 GUCCI WATCH – WHICH WAS STILL WORKING WHEN THE DOCTORS REMOVED IT!

SCIENTISTS at the University... HAVE DETERMINED THAT THE BUMP... AN ALLIGATORS FACIAL SKIN ARE SO SENSITIVE THEY CAN DETECT RIPPLES from A SINGLE DROP of WATER!
www.comics.com

IN Sapporo, Japan, THE PRICE of A SINGLE MELON AT THE MITSUKOSHI DEPARTMENT STORE IS $1,174!

A VOLCANO THAT ERUPTED in New Zealand AROUND 130 A.D. EJECTED 33 BILLION TONS of PUMICE OVER 20,000 SQUARE MILES!

8-11
Dist. by United Feature Syndicate, Inc.

Ripley's — Believe It...

THE FIRST COIN-OPERATED TELEPHONES APPEARED in 1899, BUT BEFORE THAT, PEOPLE HANDED THE MONEY TO AN ATTENDANT STANDING NEARBY!

...of Sheffield, England, HAS HER OWN INTERNET WEB SITE WHICH RECEIVES ABOUT 1000 VISITORS A DAY!

AUSTRALIAN OLYMPIC AERIAL FREESTYLE SKIER JACQUI COOPER DRANK A POTION MADE OUT of CRUSHED COCKROACHES IN DIET SODA TO HELP HER RECOVER from A BACK INJURY!

A COMPANY in Chicago, Ill., BUILT A PLAYABLE GUITAR THAT WAS 8 feet, 10 inches TALL and WEIGHED 80 LBS..! SUBMITTED BY DAN PAULIN, W. LAFAYETTE, OHIO

www.comics.com

4-28
© 2002 Ripley Entertainment Inc.
Dist. by United Feature Syndicate, Inc.

John Graziano
Ripley artist from 2004 to present day

Ripley's **Believe It or Not!**®

THE GIANT SQUID'S BRAIN IS SHAPED LIKE A DONUT AND ENCIRCLES ITS ESOPHAGUS!

Submitted By Chester Tumidajewicz, Amsterdam, N.Y.

BEAK HOUSE! CHARLES DICKENS HAD A PET RAVEN NAMED GRIP!

U.K. COMPANY **AND VINYLY** PRESSES HUMAN AND ANIMAL ASHES INTO VINYL RECORDS!

5-7 © 2016 Ripley Entertainment Inc.

www.ripleys.com

Distributed by Universal Uclick for UFS

Ripley's **Believe It or Not!**®

IN JANUARY

LICE anga, Colombia, HT A PIGEON G TO FLY UANA NE INTO RISON

www.comics.com

THE "GEREWOL COMPETITION" THE **WODAABE,** A TRIBE OF NOMADS IN NIGER, HAVE A FESTIVAL WHERE YOUNG MEN DANCE AND SING IN A BEAUTY AND TALENT CONTEST JUDGED BY THE TRIBE'S YOUNG WOMEN!

Dist. by United Feature Syndicate Inc.

© 2011 Ripley Entertainment Inc. 5-3

Ripley's **Believe It or Not!**®

SHHHH!

FOOD FOR THOUGHT!

BROOKLYN RESTAURANT "EAT" OFFERS A FOUR-COURSE DINNER THAT MUST BE EATEN IN SILENCE ...

YOU ARE MORE LIKELY TO FALL IN LOVE IN AUTUMN DUE TO CHEMICAL CHANGES IN THE BRAIN.

STACHE-ISM!

IN 1957, WALT DISNEY BANNED DISNEY EMPLOYEES FROM WEARING A MOUSTACHE — A RULE NOT DROPPED UNTIL 2000.

Submitted By Richard Gibson, Lafayette, La.

Distributed by Universal Uclick for UFS

www.gocomics.com

© 2014 Ripley Entertainment Inc. 1-1

www.ripleys.com

Ripley's **Believe It or Not!**®

TODAY ARKS THE BICENTENNIAL F THE RTH F AHAM LN

LCOLN'S U.S. GATES OO!

2-12

Dist. by United Feature Syndicate Inc.

© 2009 Ripley Entertainment Inc. www.ripleys.com

Graziano

Originally from New Jersey, John Graziano graduated from the Newark School of Fine and Industrial Art with a degree in illustration. A lifelong fan of Ripley's Believe It or Not!, he finally became the Ripley artist in 2004 and is still drawing the cartoon to this day.

Ripley's Believe It or Not!®

ONE MEDIEVAL FOLK CURE FOR JAUNDICE WAS TO DROWN EXACTLY NINE LICE IN A PINT OF BEER AND DRINK IT EVERY MORNING FOR A WEEK.

Submitted By Chester Tumidajewicz, Amsterdam, N.Y.

"FRANKENSTEIN" AUTHOR MARY SHELLEY CARRIED HER DECEASED HEART WITH HER FOR NEAR...

PUNK ROCK PUPS! PAUL AND PAMELA MOTT OF SCRIPPS RANCH, CALIFORNIA, CREATED THE SPIKED COYOTE VEST TO HELP SAVE DOGS FROM COYOTE ATTACKS.

AIN'T I PURDY?

ROSY MAPLE MOTHS, FOUND IN NORTH AMERICA, ARE...

Distributed by Universal Uclick for UFS

Ripley's Believe It or Not!®

ASTRONAUTS ON THE APOLLO MOON MISSIONS HAD VELCRO INSIDE THEIR HELMETS TO HELP THEM SCRATCH THEIR NOSES.

www.gocomics.com

MAGICIAN JAMIE D. GRANT OF VANCOUVER, CANADA, CAN MEMORIZE THE ORDER OF A SHUFFLED DECK OF CARDS IN UNDER ONE MINUTE!

VENEZUELA MADE IT A CRIME TO SELL VIOLENT VIDEO GAMES AND TOYS IN 2009— PUNISHABLE BY 5 YEARS IN JAIL.

2-9 © 2015 Ripley Entertainment Inc.

Distributed by Universal Uclick for UFS

Ripley's Believe It or Not!®

THE LARGEST OF EASTER ISLAND'S ANCIENT MOAI STATUES WEIGHS MORE THAN 80 TONS!

Submitted By Bobby Owens, Myrtle Beach, S.C., USA.

Dist. by United Feature Syndicate Inc.

JACKIE ROBINSON WAS NOT ONLY THE FIRST BLACK MAJOR LEAGUE BASEBALL PLAYER — BUT HE WAS ALSO THE LEAGUE'S FIRST RO... OF THE YEAR!

Submitted By Bobby Owens, Myrtle Beach...

WELCOME TO WAUCONDA

The Researchers

How does the longest syndicated cartoon in history still produce a cartoon a day?

1. Norbert Pearlroth 1923–1975
2. Charles Grant 1976–1989
3. Karen Kemlo 1989–2004
4. Lucas Stram 2004–2012
5. James Proud 2012–2014
6. Sabrina Sieck 2014–present

After Ripley hired Norbert Pearlroth in 1923, the team grew to include a crew of employees behind the scenes. Secretaries and assistants who handled everything from fact checking to opening Ripley's constant stream of mail helped Pearlroth stay afloat, pushing out unbelievable toons that provoked and astounded readers.

Today, as when Ripley was alive, a team of editors and fact checkers assists in the production of the strip— and the company still has a lead researcher who finds all the incredible facts and stories that make up the daily cartoon. Only five people since Pearlroth have held the position. Norbert Pearlroth remains the longest-reigning lead researcher and longest Ripley's Believe It or Not! employee, staying 53 years at his post.

Norbert Pearlroth 1923–1975

BELIEVE IT OR NOT! LEGENDARY RIPLEY'S RESEARCHER NORBERT PEARLROTH, FLUENT IN 14 LANGUAGES, READ 350,000 BOOKS IN 52 YEARS AND SPENT NEARLY EVERY DAY FROM 1923 TO 1975 IN THE READING ROOM OF THE NEW YORK PUBLIC LIBRARY!

Karen Kemlo 1989-2004

I started working at Ripley's after graduating from journalism school at Ryerson University in Toronto. I answered an ad in the local newspaper and was interviewed by Edward Meyer. I'd read the books and cartoon for years as a kid and had always loved the column.

After I got the job, I spent a lot of time in libraries, scouring newspapers and magazines—when I started, the Internet was not around! I always loved the historical cartoons—the ones that featured people walking backward across America or building a string ball that was bigger than a house. I love the sense of wonder and whimsy. I also loved unusual hobbies, like the woman who created life-size sculptures out of laundry lint. Stories of survival are also some of my faves, like the man who survived being shot after the bullet lodged in a huge wad of losing lottery tickets.

There's a few funny stories during my first years at Ripley's. We received a rusty screw in the mail from a man in Sweden who claimed it had been up his nose for over 20 years and only came out when he sneezed. That was a bit gross. We also received some carefully wrapped stones—actually kidney stones—from a man and his wife who claimed that if you looked closely you could see their initials in each! It was highly weird and amusing.

I think I am most proud of the fact that in 15 years I researched, fact checked, and wrote over 21,000 Believe It or Not! stories. I loved how Ripley's has such devoted, loyal fans. It's something that spans generations, I think. And I appreciate how it has always embraced the weird and the wonderful, the imaginative and the downright bizarre, too.

> "In journalism school, I did stories on eccentric people, tattoo artists, and even a man who kept lions and tigers in a former corner grocery store in Toronto."
>
> — Karen Kemlo

Lucas Stram 2004–2012

Unfortunately, this is a story of failure. The butcher could only get me a box of four frozen pig heads, not a single pig head, so I thawed the box of frozen heads in my friend's fridge for three days. When I finally took the heads out of the box, the cheeks were cut off the pigs' heads, so I couldn't do it!

"If you spend time studying another culture, it gives you a good sense of how much is going on in the world beyond just your own bubble, which is one thing I appreciated about this job—the chance to constantly learn."
— Lucas Stram

I studied political science and east Asian studies in school, and actually spent two semesters in China. When I graduated, I was looking for work and I saw the position was available. I didn't know a ton about Ripley's, but I had seen the Dean Cain shows and been to the museum in St. Augustine. Norm Deska hired me and a couple other people to do it part-time, but in the end, I ended up taking it on as a full-time thing.

We had a bunch of regular contributors; for instance, there was an award-winning Pakistani civic engineer who would write to us about world events. Working with John Graziano was great. There's so many little things that go into making the cartoon, and for John, this is craft. He believes in it in a way that I don't think a lot of people appreciate.

I've always enjoyed eclectic, weird stuff, and Ripley's has that. One of the common Ripley's motifs is the shrunken head, so one time I took it upon myself to give it a try. I collected the rocks, made sure I had some nice, clean sand for it, asked a friend if I could use his fire pit, and talked to a butcher to get some pig heads.

LUKE STRAM - RESEARCH "THE BRAINS OF THE OPERATION"!

Ripley's — Believe It or Not!®

Ye Olde
Research
Department
Master James Proud

"PROUD TO
BE ONBOARD"
JAMES
PROUD,
of Saffron Walden,
England,
HAS TAKEN ON THE ENVIABLE
SITUATION OF BECOMING THE
LATEST RESEARCHER OF THE
WORLD FAMOUS
Ripley's — Believe It or Not!
CARTOON FEATURE!
WELCOME, JAMES!

James Proud 2012–2014

I first started as a picture researcher, finding weird and wonderful images for the annual Ripley's book, and then I eventually started writing the cartoon. Before I joined the company, I had heard of Ripley's Believe It or Not! from the TV show, but I didn't know much about Robert Ripley's incredible history.

I'm most proud of being one of the few people tasked with writing the long-running *Believe It or Not!* cartoon. My favorite cartoon is probably the one featuring myself that John Graziano kindly drew for me! I have many amusing stories from my time at Ripley's, but I do fondly remember the book 7, *Enter If You Dare!*, launch at the London Museum. Not many people can say that they have met the smallest man in the world!

Sabrina Sieck 2014–Present

SABRINA

There was a closeness to those tapes, to that reading room, that made me feel like I was experiencing history in real time. A closeness that I'm sure Norbert Pearlroth felt as he traveled the world from behind the stacks of the New York Public Library.

Like Norbert, I ended up in New York. Bouncing from newsroom to newsroom, it was the city that built my sense of wonder. I began antiquing for rare finds, collecting taxidermy and tattoos, and exploring the little-known corners of the city. From eating adventurously to visiting holy relics at the Church of the Most Holy Redeemer, New York began to build my BION library.

In 2014, the role of Ripley's researcher was brought to my attention, but it was headquartered in my hometown of Orlando, Florida. I begrudgingly realized it was time to go back home.

Now, after five years on the job, the role of Ripley Researcher has evolved. With a brain full of the bizarre, I now present my research not only in print but also digitally, hosting shows on YouTube and acting as a sounding board for all online content. Another shift in this role can be attributed to the company's strong editorial staff. With the Ripley Publishing team contributing to research efforts, we leave no strange stone unturned! This collaboration champions our company culture of curiosity and, on a closer level, welcomes some unprecedented cubical conversations.

Returning to Florida was the right decision, although, believe it or not, I still have never been to Maine.

In elementary school, I tried to get away with doing every research report on the state of Maine or anacondas (presumably due to my love of lobster and the 1997 box-office hit). It wasn't until journalism school at George Washington University that my passion for digging deep into the facts came along.

There, I learned the tricks of investigative journalism (now Catfishing 101) and spent some serious time sorting through the National Archives. Locked away in a reading room day after day, I put on headphones, inserted a tape into a dated machine, pressed play, and was transported back to the 1970s. I was transcribing the Nixon White House tapes, waiting for that Believe It or Not! moment to report.

WOMEN IN CAKES

LEECH FACIAL

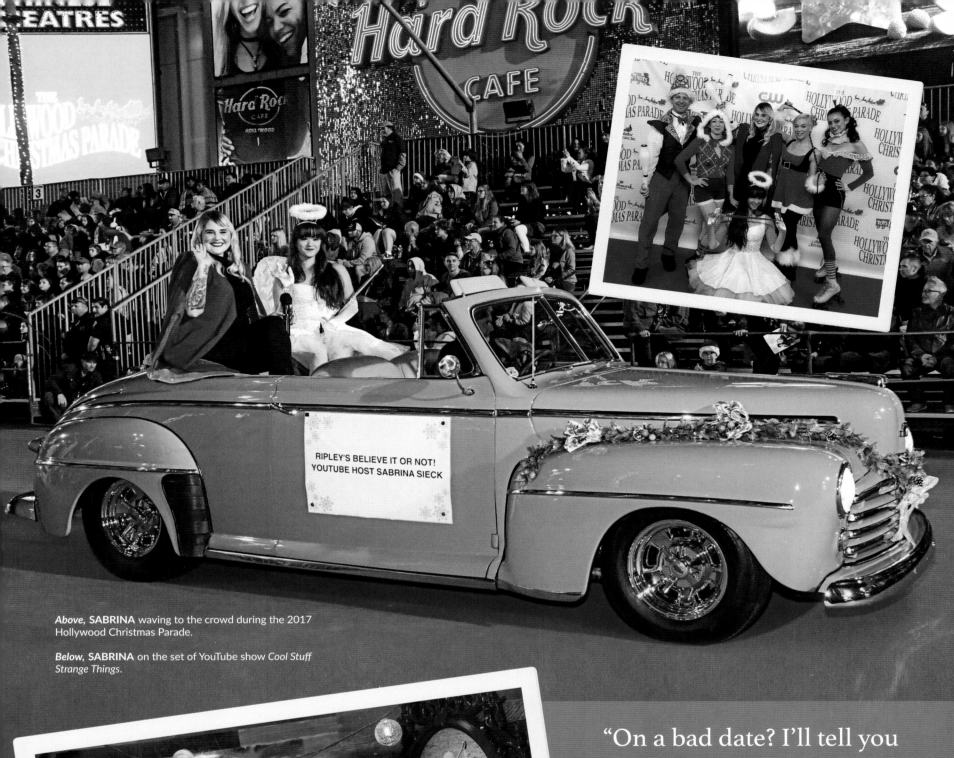

Above, **SABRINA** waving to the crowd during the 2017 Hollywood Christmas Parade.

Below, **SABRINA** on the set of YouTube show *Cool Stuff Strange Things*.

RIPLEY'S BELIEVE IT OR NOT!
YOUTUBE HOST SABRINA SIECK

"On a bad date? I'll tell you what a 35-year-old collection of belly button lint smells like! There is a BION for every social situation, and I have become the ultimate source for cocktail party conversations."

Media

Foreword by Norm Deska

Below, **AT EDGEWALK** at Toronto's CN Tower during a manager's meeting.

Robert Ripley was one of the most cutting-edge figures of the 20th century—he pioneered bringing the world to the masses via newspaper, radio, and television. He was a blogger long before blogging was a thing. And he has given us extraordinary content that stands out in the entertainment industry still today.

I started working for a public accounting firm in Toronto in 1979, and the very first client that ever walked in the door was Ripley's Believe It or Not! I knew little about accounting, but I did know that I liked this funky little company with its fascinating product and entrepreneurial spirit. After being on the annual audit for three years, I made the jump to working for Ripley's.

From my position as vice president of finance, I moved over to operations, running all of our attractions, and then I moved on to franchising. It was such an exciting time, opening new attractions all over the world with Bob Masterson. Perhaps my favorite times in my decades with the company revolve around travel—like drinking snake blood in Taipei, being attacked by a monkey in Malaysia, or getting stranded overnight at the airport in Tallinn, Estonia, with no heat and only the light from a Coke machine. Without a visa, I was unable to either enter the country or buy a ticket to leave it, just like that guy from the movie *The Terminal.*

My role in intellectual property and media evolved out of operations. At that time, our licensing agent was Bob Whiteman. He was the only guy I ever met who had actually met Robert Ripley. Apart from TV, his book publishing deals were probably the most successful. The books with Simon & Schuster, Scholastic, and J. P. Leventhal—all of those were licensing agreements.

It wasn't until around 2003 that we got into publishing for ourselves. A distributor by the name of Morty Mint called me up saying he thought that Ripley could be as strong as Guinness World Records in the market, and he convinced me that the company should self-publish an annual book. The first edition sold well over 500,000 copies, and we built the program from there.

In the beginning, we contracted with Miles Kelly Publishing in the United Kingdom to package the book. They did a great job, but we soon realized that to really have control and be able to invest in our product we needed to bring production in house. Anne Marshall and her team at Miles were really committed to the brand, and with Miles Kelly's cooperation, we were able to nicely transition the team, and that's how our little publishing office ended up in the United Kingdom. Anne and her team created the book for about 10 years, up until she decided to retire, and then the decision was made to move the operation here to Orlando.

I think when anyone thinks of Ripley in media, the TV shows automatically come to mind, and there's been a few of them over the years. There are the Vitaphone shorts and the original Ripley show that Ripley had a heart attack on. They kept the show going for a couple years without Ripley. Then the Jack Palance show came along. People loved Jack, and still do, because he was that "creepy guy." He embodied the brand so well. The day the first episode aired, our museums' attendance went up by 25 percent—just like bang! It was amazing. It became a new plateau for the brand.

Our next show was hosted by Dean Cain—you know, Superman—and Kelly Packard from *Baywatch*. That show almost didn't happen. After some long negotiations, deal fatigue had settled in and Sony was ready to walk away. To Bob Whiteman's credit, he convinced Andy Kaplan (the president of Sony Television) to clear one afternoon to meet with Bob and me with the understanding that by the end of the meeting we would either complete the deal or kill it. It's amazing what focus and a deadline will do. The hour-long show ran for four seasons, and today, some 15 years later, it's still being syndicated in countries around the world.

The scope of our media presence has changed dramatically from when I started my career with Ripley's. The Internet didn't exist; the Ripley's researchers were still combing the public library like Norbert Pearlroth did. We've evolved from one-way communication, with Ripley inserting stories and images from fan letters into the cartoon, to being an aggregator of unbelievable content for people. It makes our jobs easier in some respects and more difficult in others.

It's a fun industry to be sure, but I love that Ripley's is still run as a small entrepreneurial company. Our company culture has always been one of *work hard, play harder*. When I look back on all the accomplishments of the company, of the teams that I have been a part of, built, and managed, I'm in awe. It's been a wild ride and by being able to move from job to job, all within the same company, I've been given the opportunity to pursue my interests.

I am looking forward to the future, to what the new digital age holds for the brand and its continual growth.

Above top, **AMANDA JOINER**, Norm, and Anne Marshall in Bologna, Italy.

Above bottom, **NORM** with Lizardman.

Left, **NORM** and Bob Masterson in costume at a Partners in Pride annual manager's meeting in 1987.

Vitaphone

R ipley made his way onto the big screen when he signed a lucrative deal with Warner Bros. to star in "Vitaphone Varieties" shows.

The film shorts proved a boon for Ripley. Viewers wanted to see his odd guest performers, curiosities, and personal travel footage, as well as watch the famed cartoonist sketch them right before their eyes.

THE NAME "Vitaphone" is derived from the Latin word *vita* meaning "living" and the Greek word *phone* meaning "sound."

Left, **THEATER** marquee introducing Ripley's Vitaphone segment along with film star James Cagney's latest movie, *Blonde Crazy*, released in 1931.

Below, **PROMOTIONAL** poster for Ripley's Vitaphone Varieties series.

In the very first Vitaphone short, Ripley draws One Long Hop, a Chinese boy who was named in honor of Lindbergh. As the camera focuses on his intricate drawing, One Long Hop materializes right before the audience's eyes. Ripley then seemingly pulls One Long Hop right off the page for a quick song from the child. He ends the segment saying, "I'm gonna put you right back in the paper," and so he does.

Below top, **ONE LONG HOP** posing with Ripley and his detailed sketch.

Below bottom, **THE ORIGINAL** cartoon of One Long Hop when he was still an infant, released October 18, 1927.

A CHINESE BABY — born
in Chicago — WAS NAMED AFTER LINDBERGH
They called him: "ONE LONG HOP"
Born Sept 14, 1927

In another episode, Ripley drew the "Lighthouse Man"—a tour guide from Chungking, China, who once guided American dignitaries through the streets of Chungking by the light of a candle in his head! Today the Lighthouse Man is immortalized in almost every Odditorium as a wax figure.

THE
HORNED
MAN!

Jeremiah Disle - of the
MAYATOS KRAAL
HAS A HORN ON HIS HEAD
11½ INCHES LONG.

He has shed 4 horns!
- is 32 yrs old &
and is coming to
America

HACK
WILSON
Heavy Hitter
of the CUBS
FANNED
6 TIMES
IN SUCCESSION
July 22-23
1929
Cubs vs Giants
New York

A. HAILSTONE 17 INCHES
IN DIAMETER FELL AT POTTER, Neb.
July 6, 1928.

A CAT MOTHERED A LITTER OF MICE
she accidentally raised them
to maturity. — Oslo, Norway.

Above, **THE CARTOON** for "the Horned Man" appeared on August 17, 1929, which was originally published in black and white.

Right, **LIU CH'UNG,** the four-eyed man from China, was featured in Ripley's 1929 *Believe It or Not!* best-selling book.

Below, **WITH TWO** pupils in each eye, Ch'ung's wax figure makes an appearance at several Odditoriums around the world.

BELIEVE IT OR NOT

THE HALF WOMAN

"VIOLETTA," as she prefers to be known, was born without arms or legs, of normal parents less than thirty years ago in Germany. She is a lady of perennial good nature—realizing that what one never possesses one never misses. Her body is well formed otherwise, she enjoys perfect health, and her senses of sight, hearing, smell, taste and touch are all developed and perfected in their separate and various functions far beyond the average normal person's.

Violetta's accomplishments in overcoming the unkindness of Mother Nature are astounding. She rarely needs the assistance of anyone, and is able to get about with remarkable facility. She can dress herself, comb her own hair, thread a needle, sew, and perform other feats apparently bordering on the impossible.

94

BELIEVE IT OR NOT

LIU CH'UNG

HAD DOUBLE EYES

THE DOUBLE-EYED MAN

LIU CH'UNG, or Liu Min, as he was sometimes known, was born with double pupils in each eye. This strange freak of nature did not in the least deter this active man. He became Governor of Shansi, Minister of State, and through intrigue with the Dowager Empress, had his son proclaimed Heir Apparent. He also loved wine and gambling.

I refer you to Herbert A. Giles' book on China.

THE MAN WITHOUT EARS

EZECHIEL EADS, of Athens, New York, who died in 1884, was born without ears. The sides of his head bore no trace of ears whatever; neither had he openings for ears. However, he was able to hear through his mouth which he opened wide for the purpose.

99

Radio

Ripley signed with NBC in the 1930s, making his official foray into the world of radio.

As with Vitaphone, Ripley introduced listeners to the real-life "believe it or nots" he had been featuring in his cartoons for years—the speed-talker, a man who survived being buried alive, or a legless swimmer.

"It makes me very happy to be a success in radio, for it's the last thing I'd ever imagine I could do."
—Robert Ripley

Far Left, RIPLEY interviewed "El Fusilado," or "the Executed One," on his program, July 16, 1937. The man, Wenseslao Moguel, survived a firing squad, receiving eight bullets through the head and body plus the *coup de grace* (or the kill shot). Moguel also appeared at the 1937 Cleveland Odditorium.

Left, RIPLEY standing with billiard ball manipulator Julius Schuster, a.k.a. the "Pick-Up Artist," who is holding 20 balls in one hand. Schuster appeared at numerous Odditoriums, in several cartoons, and in a Vitaphone film.

Right, RIPLEY with Colombian singer Sarita Herrera playing the maracas, circa late 1930s.

TONIGHT AT 7:45

"Believe it or Not"

Ripley

WILL BROADCAST FROM MID-OCEAN

the first of a bi-weekly series of radio programs featuring the new incredible truths he is bringing back from his 2½-month tour of Africa and Europe. The first ship-to-shore broadcast by a radio star ever attempted—don't miss it!

$5,000.00 Prize Contest
FOR YOUR "BELIEVE IT OR NOT" IDEAS

Tune in and hear also how you can win big rewards offered by the manufacturers of Esso, world's leading motor car fuel. Entry blanks at all service stations selling Esso.

EVERY WEDNESDAY AND FRIDAY **WJZ**

THE NEW *Esso* ENTERTAINMENT

Admit One - Oct 11
Compliments of
ROYAL CROWN
194

Ripley's 17-year run on radio included major accomplishments in broadcasting:

1926   Transmitted a cartoon from London to New York

1931   Broadcast from ship to shore

1932   Broadcast from Australia to New York

1934   Broadcast the first radio program heard simultaneously around the world

1939   Broadcast from underground

1940   Broadcast from underwater

Left, **DURING** a live May 31, 1940, radio broadcast, Ripley talks to a parachutist in midair over an Alabama airshow.

Below, **NEHI NEWS** reporting on Ripley's radio broadcast from Marineland, Florida, March 1940.

NEHI NEWS

MARCH, 1940

Volume 2, No. 2

Columbus, Ga.

RADIO PROGRAM HITS NEW POPULARITY PEAK

After a series of spectacular broadcasts, which moved at a fast clip, ROYAL CROWN'S CBS 88-station coast-to-coast radio program featuring "Believe-It-Or-Not" Bob Ripley has hit a new popularity peak. Following the opener in New York February 16th, Ripley and the cast sojourned to Florida, where two outstanding programs were broadcast. The listening audience has steadily increased and the program is now rated one of the top half-hour shows on the air.

Stimulated by scores of favorable program reviews, which include the prized Variety and Radio Daily columns, and innumerable letters and gratifying expressions from ROYAL CROWN Bottlers, the cast is determined to march the program to an even greater height.

The St. Augustine, Florida, "Marine Studio" program was heralded a broadcast triumph by many radio columnists, and proved an exciting venture for Bob Ripley and the listeners. The daring presentation won a number of hearty program endorsements and many letters stated that ROYAL CROWN was putting thrill into radio listening.

In pictorial form we review the highlights of the program broadcast from Marineland—located near St. Augustine, Florida.

TOO LATE NOW! Bob Ripley dons the diver's suit . . . willingly but not enthusiastically.

TO SHARK-INFESTED WATERS! Down in the deep he goes to tell the world how it feels to meet a man-eating shark face to face.

A HUNGRY PORPOISE FED BY HAND! Lurching forward at great speed, the mammal feeds from human hands.

WE'RE ON THE AIR! Action and thrills are sent through these radio engineers to over a million listening radio fans.

Ripley's EST. 1918

With Doug Storer taking the reins on Ripley's radio career, things started to heat up when on-location broadcasting bloomed.

The ambitious duo pioneered reality radio—interviewing such guests as "The Modern Adam and Eve," a couple that married after the man donated a rib to help surgeons repair the woman's injuries after a car accident—and started making headlines with their wild stunt-driven *See America First with Bob Ripley* broadcasts.

Below and right, **ON JUNE 2, 1939,** Ripley took his show 750 feet belowground to New Mexico's Carlsbad Caverns. The broadcast was also made into a Movietone newsreel.

This page, **ON AUGUST 2, 1938**, Indian "mystic" Kuda Bux walked barefoot across a bed of hot coals. Hundreds of onlookers were present, and a team of doctors were on hand to examine Kuda's feet before and after the stunt. The man emerged unscathed.

Above, **RIPLEY** was the first to broadcast underwater with his Marineland stunt in St. Augustine, Florida, on February 23, 1940. He milked a porpoise on-air and then spoke from inside his diving suit in a huge tank containing sharks and porpoises.

This page, **AT SILVER SPRINGS STATE PARK** in Silver Springs, Florida, Ripley milked a rattlesnake on-air. A mishap occurred when Ripley climbed into a pit with 500 rattlesnakes with proprietor Ross Allen and the lights went out, prompting the professional snake handler to scream "Let's get the hell outta here!" on-air.

"MILKING" A RATTLESNAKE
Ripley's
BELIEVE IT or NOT PROGRAM
Sunday — MAY 17, 1935
NBC   BLUE NETWORK

ALLEN   RIPLEY

"Don't be frightened by that noise you hear in the background. It is just the bellowing of the alligators, who are all excited by this broadcast from their homeland!"
—Ripley on the May 17, 1935, broadcast

RIPLEY "BELIEVE IT ~ or NOT

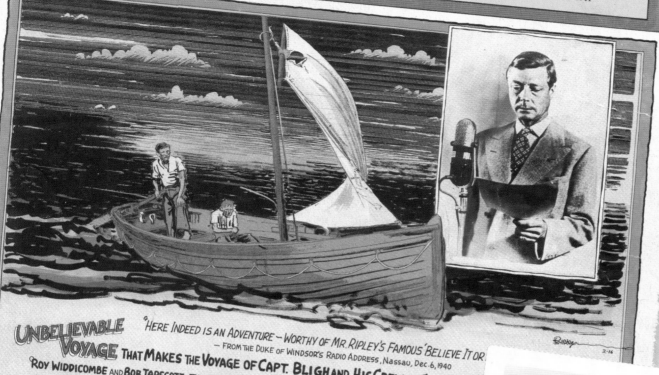

Believe It or Not

By Ripley

Most Amazing Voyage Of All Time
SUNDAY, FEBRUARY 16, 1941

UNBELIEVABLE VOYAGE "HERE INDEED IS AN ADVENTURE – WORTHY OF MR. RIPLEY'S FAMOUS 'BELIEVE IT OR..."
— FROM THE DUKE OF WINDSOR'S RADIO ADDRESS, NASSAU, DEC. 6, 1940

THAT MAKES THE VOYAGE OF CAPT. BLIGH AND HIS CREW OF CASTAWAYS

ROY WIDDICOMBE AND BOB TAPSCOTT – TORPEDOED BRITISH SEAM...

CAPT. BLIGH'S VOYAGE TOOK 41 DAYS...

WIDDICOMBE AND TAPSCO...

...OF THE PERILOUS ATLANT...

...PPED FOR NAVIGATION. B...

...D FOR NAVIGATION, AM...

Left, ON DECEMBER 6, 1940, the Duke of Windsor appeared on Ripley's program, the first time British "royalty" was on a commercial radio show. He read a short prepared speech after Ripley interviewed Roy Widdicombe and Robert Tapscott—two sailors who survived at sea after their cargo ship was torpedoed by Germans off the coast of Africa.

Ripley marked the occasion with a cartoon that appeared on February 16, 1941.

Below, FOR THE MAY 17, 1940, Grand Canyon broadcast, it took 30 mules to carry actors, writers, guides, and 2,000 pounds of equipment down to the canyon floor.

The First Show

Starting a weekly television show in the spring of 1949 was just icing on the cake for Ripley—he had already earned well over half-a-million dollars a year during the height of the Depression.

It was one of the very first weekly television shows. Airing on NBC, Ripley appeared in the first 13 episodes, which included him showing guests his exotic artifacts and drawing cartoons for the camera, reenactments of "believe it or not" stories, and interviews with the real-life "stars" of the stories.

On show #13 on May 23, 1949, Ripley had a heart attack while on stage discussing the military funeral hymn "Taps." He recovered enough to finish the show, but checked into a hospital the next morning and died there three days later. The 14th episode was a eulogy.

The television show continued on for more than two years, hosted by a man named Robert St. John and Ripley's close friend Li Ling Ai.

*Below, **RIPLEY** on screen as the host of his own TV show.*

TBS ORIGINAL PRODUCTION

THE INCREDIBLE LIFE AND TIMES OF

Robert Ripley
Believe It or Not!

RIPLEY was the first person ever to broadcast, via radio, to every nation in the world simultaneously. He used a corps of translators to accomplish this remarkable feat.

RIPLEY received more mail than anyone in history. One contest alone—a mere 14-day period—netted him **OVER 2,000,000 LETTERS!**

A SCULPTURE OF RIPLEY WAS DONE IN 1937 BY Mark Shoesmith—WHO WAS TOTALLY BLIND!

THE MODERN MARCO POLO

Charles Shulz, the creator of the PEANUTS comic strip published his first drawing of a Ripley cartoon—when he was only 12 years old.

ON ONE OF HIS MANY EXPEDITIONS, RIPLEY TRAVELED 24,000 MILES—15,000 BY AIR, 8,000 BY SHIP, AND 1,000 BY CAMEL, DONKEY AND HORSE!

MAN or IMAGE? RIPLEY CONSIDERED THIS TO BE AMONG HIS GREATEST FINDS! JAPANESE ARTIST Hananuma Masakichi CREATED THIS AMAZING SELF PORTRAIT. THE SCULPTURE IS ANATOMICALLY CORRECT DOWN TO THE TINIEST DETAILS, AND INCLUDES THE ARTIST'S OWN HAIR AND FINGERNAILS!

FRIDAY, NOVEMBER 26th 8:30 pm/et **TBS** SUPERSTATION

Below, **HOST ROBERT ST. JOHN** and Li Ling Ai featured in an episode. Ripley's Believe It or Not! Inc. president Doug Storer made a cameo on the show with a watch he purchased for the "believe it or not" story behind it.

RIPLEY'S
Believe it
or Not!

Produced by
Truman Talley

Presenting

BOB RIPLEY . . . . Himself
RICHARD KOLLMAR . . . . . Wm. Westover
LISTER CHAMBERS . . . . . Judge Gary
WALTER SCOTT WEEKS . . . Mr. McAllen
LINDA BISHOP . . . . Helen Wade
DANIEL HAYES . . . . Judge Thompson
JAMES O'NEIL . . . . Judge Blake
HERBERT STANDING . . . . London Bobby
HAROLD DE BECKER . . . . Court Guard
also ships crew, passengers, survivors,
dock attendants, derelicts and police.

the newest—most
exciting half hour
on TELEVISION
RIPLEY'S
Believe
It or Not!
featuring ROBERT L. RIPLEY in person

tonite 9 P. M. station WDTV channel 3
presented by Motorola
RADIO TELEVISION

comedy   thrills   variety   drama

Hosted by Jack Palance

From 1981 to 1986, the *Ripley's Believe It or Not!* TV show aired on ABC, famously hosted by actor Jack Palance and his daughter Holly Palance.

Former Ripley president John Withers and longtime Ripley licensing agent Bob Whiteman were instrumental in making sure negotiations resulted in a TV show.

Licensed to Raystar Television Inc., this revival of the original *Ripley's Believe It or Not!* television show starting in 1949 was such a success that it increased the revenue at every Odditorium and left a lasting impression on the pop culture consciousness of a generation.

Right, **JACK** with the "auto-icon" of Jeremy Bentham, who attended board meetings at the University College London. After death, Bentham left instructions for his body, but the mummification of his head went awry. This "mummy" is actually Bentham's skeleton, stuffed with hay and adorned with his clothes, and a wax replica of his head.

JACK on set at the St. Augustine Odditorium with licensing agent Bob Whiteman, former Ripley's president John Withers, and producer Jack Haley Jr.

Former Ripley president John Withers tells more:

The Jack Palance TV show originally started out with Columbia Pictures approaching us to do a movie on the life of Robert Ripley. We negotiated a contract but a deal never materialized. They fortunately gave up the rights. At just about the same time *Real People* and *That's Incredible!* became successful on television, somebody had the bright idea, "Well, if these can work, then Ripley certainly could work."

Columbia came to us to negotiate getting the rights back again, and this time it only took about three or four months. Columbia Pictures had real control. We had the right to talk to them about their plans, but we couldn't overrule something that they decided they wanted to do. They came up with several ideas on who the lead should be, and Jack Palance was one of them.

Bob Whiteman was involved through this piece in helping me decide where we had to be tough and where we could be a little easier in negotiating these contracts.

JACK at the cathedral of bones, Sedlec Ossuary, in Kutná Hora, Czech Republic.

Above, PROMO poster

"People remember the hosts—Dean Cain and Jack Palance, who is my personal favorite. Palance just embodied the brand with his persona. He just got it. The Palance show had the right vibe to it. The way he could say 'believe it or not' was very unique."
—Jim Pattison Jr., President of Ripley Entertainment

Initially, the show began as two hour-long pilot episodes called "specials" before it was picked up for 3½ seasons. It was later cohosted by Catherine Shirriff and singer Marie Osmond.

Top left, **CATHERINE SHIRRIFF** poses on set, circa 1982–83.

Bottom left, **JACK AND HOLLY** Palance pose with the wax museum cast of *The Wizard of Oz* at the Movieland Wax Museum.

Center, **PROMO** illustration by Robert Bentovoja.

PALANCE in Sherwood Forest, Nottingham, for the segment "In Search of Robin Hood."

HERE LIES
LESTER MOORE
FOUR SLUGS
FROM A-44
NO LES
NO MORE

Left, **PALANCE** with producer Jack Haley Jr. at Boot Hill Cemetery for the May 1981 special.

Above left, bottom right, **JACK** on set dressed for a reenactment.

Animated Series

Ripley's long history of cartoons gained a new outlet with *Ripley's Believe It or Not! The Animated Series*, which ran from July 1999 to 2000.

Licensed and produced by Cinar Productions Inc., the show aired on the Fox Family Channel and consisted of 30-minute episodes, with a total of 26 episodes.

It featured three people—Robert Ripley's fictional nephew Michael (nicknamed "Rip") and his companions Samantha and Cyril—on their globe-trotting adventures to discover unexplained mysteries and unusual artifacts. The character Cyril was modeled after Ripley researchers past and present, with his brainy personality and his job researching for Michael.

Ripley's Believe It or Not!

Hosted by Dean Cain

From 2000 to 2003, a new Ripley's Believe It or Not! show starring Dean Cain took prime time by storm... Viewer discretion advised.

Running for four seasons and a total of 88 hour-long episodes, the show first aired on TBS and was hosted by Dean Cain of *Superman* fame, as well as Kelly Packard from *Baywatch*.

Ripley's Believe It or Not!®
Wednesdays 8pm ET / 7pm PT
TBS SUPERSTATION

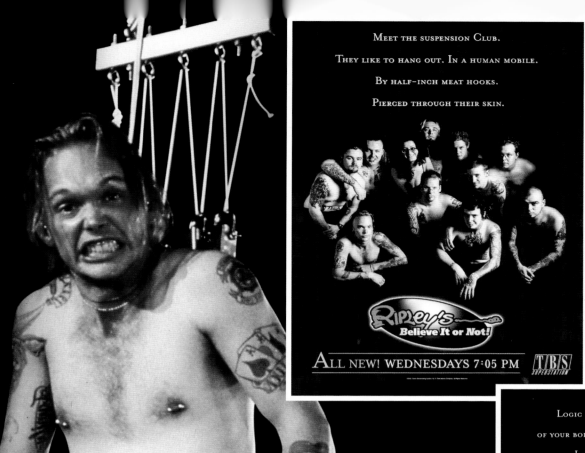

MEET THE SUSPENSION CLUB.

THEY LIKE TO HANG OUT. IN A HUMAN MOBILE.

BY HALF-INCH MEAT HOOKS.

PIERCED THROUGH THEIR SKIN.

Ripley's Believe It or Not!

ALL NEW! WEDNESDAYS 7:05 PM **T/B/S** SUPERSTATION

On January 12, 2000, Season 1, Episode 1 started the show off with a bang as the memorable Suspension Club wowed the audience by doing what they do best—spinning in a human mobile while hanging from half-inch meat hooks pierced through their skin. Location: St. Augustine Odditorium

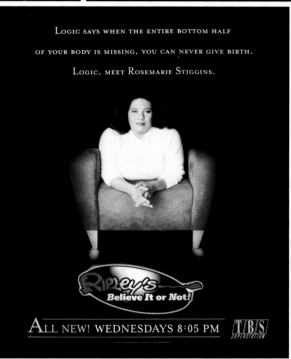

LOGIC SAYS WHEN THE ENTIRE BOTTOM HALF

OF YOUR BODY IS MISSING, YOU CAN NEVER GIVE BIRTH.

LOGIC, MEET ROSEMARIE STIGGINS.

Ripley's Believe It or Not!

ALL NEW! WEDNESDAYS 8:05 PM **T/B/S** SUPERSTATION

Among other things (like modern-day cannibals and a talking dog), the episode also featured Rosemarie Stiggins—a half-woman from Colorado who miraculously gave birth, defying logic and doctor's orders.

Robert Whiteman
Creative Consultant
Ripley Entertainment, Inc.

CLOSING credits for Season 4, Episode 11

"Bob thought that the Ripley oddities were great and that they would be wonderful in a television show. Bob had a big hand in the Palance show and the second television show with Dean Cain. He was very happy when he got the programs going. Bob was creative and colorful and had a lot of excitement for it."

—Mrs. Betty Whiteman

The show broke new ground, introducing a whole new generation to the brand.

To this day, scores of fans remember the show and recall their favorite and most memorable moments, such as these. Since 2003, the show has been successfully syndicated around the world.

Season 1, Episode 3

Season 1, Episode 3

Things heated up when Wally Glenn, a.k.a. Pyro Boy, walked through flaming rings wearing a suit covered in explosive devices. The suit ignited after his second walk-through, creating a firework bonanza. Location: Ripley's Aquarium of Myrtle Beach

Season 3, Episode 4

January 30, 2002, saw Danielle Stampe, otherwise known as Miss Electra, electrocuted with 750,000 volts of electricity and survive. Location: Hollywood Odditorium

Season 3, Episode 4

I used to eat my hair the way I used to eat my food.

I have never seen this much size of a hairball.

Unbelievable

The show detailed the shocking story of a 15-year-old girl who had a giant 3-pound hairball removed from her stomach after she was rushed to the hospital complaining of stomach pain.

Season 4, Episode 11

The episode that aired on March 19, 2003, showcased the world's largest rubber band ball, made up of 6 million rubber bands and weighing 2,600 pounds, as it was dropped from an airplane.

Publishing

Ripley Entertainment has enjoyed a long, proud publishing history, beginning all the way back with Robert Ripley's best-selling first book in 1929.

To this day, the company continues to produce a full list of titles that engage and amaze adults and children alike.

Left, **RIPLEY** on the publication day of his second *Believe It or Not!* book.

This page, **RIPLEY** stands in front of a giant replica of his second book, *The New Believe It or Not!*, released in 1931, which followed the same format as his first book.

Book Licensing

From the time of Robert Ripley's death in 1949 up to 2004, Ripley Entertainment has relied on licensing deals to fuel book publishing based on the Ripley's Believe It or Not! brand.

Working with packagers and distributors such as Simon & Schuster, Ripley's has been able to release a plethora of titles on a variety of topics and stories all centered around a common theme—things incredibly hard to believe but undeniably true, "believe it or not!"

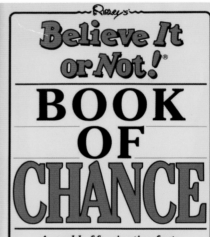

Below, **CONSISTING** of cartoon compilations, the Ripley's Believe It or Not! Pocket Books series was consistently published as a mass market paperback from 1950 to 1982.

Above, **THE 1956** *Ripley's Believe It or Not! Animal Book* by Simon & Schuster and the 1957 *Wonder Book of Facts* by Standard Home Library are two of the rarest Ripley books.

Above, **IN 1982,** *Ripley's Believe It or Not! Book of Chance* was produced by Ripley Books, a new and short-lived division of then Ripley International Limited, and published by William Collins Sons & Co.

Below, **BETWEEN** 1966 and 1976, more than 90 editions of *Ripley's Believe It or Not! True War Stories*, *True Ghosts Stories*, and *True Demons and Monsters* were published by Gold Key Comics.

ROBERT AITKEN of SAN FRANCISCO could take off his hat with a doubled-back arm. (November 22, 1938)

F. VELEZ CAMPOS, dislocationist, strikes a peculiar pose in Fortuna, PUERTO RICO. (September 23, 1933)

Above, **IN 1993,** Ripley Entertainment released *Dear Mr. Ripley,* the first Ripley book with photos rather than drawings.

A New Era

I n 2004, Ripley Publishing was launched with the successful *New York Times* bestseller *Ripley's Believe It or Not!*

Without an in-house publishing division, Ripley Entertainment hired book-packaging company Miles Kelly in the United Kingdom for the job. Miles Kelly then assigned publisher Anne Marshall to head up the project, so Anne and her team put together the very first *Ripley's Believe It or Not!* book.

Over the next few years, Miles Kelly's involvement transitioned into Anne Marshall and her UK-based team becoming a permanent part of the Ripley's Intellectual Property division, building the now in-house Ripley Publishing program from the ground up.

"We printed about 550,000 units and sold it in the market. Back then, I never really appreciated that the book could have been a failure and all those copies could have come back to us. But it had absolutely remarkable sell-through—like it was just *Wow*. And now we had no choice. We are in the publishing business."

—Norm Deska, VP of Intellectual Property

THE BOOK'S popularity led to the creation of a legacy book series released every year with all new content. The annual *Ripley's Believe It or Not!* book is also translated into dozens of languages and published in foreign markets.

Below, **THE UK TEAM** began the Twist books, an award-winning children's reference series complete with a Ripley's twist.

Above, **ANNE MARSHALL** illustrated by John Graziano

The first year was very challenging, just doing it on my own with one part-time assistant. No one ever anticipated that it was going to sell so many books. I wasn't worried, until they said half a million copies and I thought—*this is going to be something really big.* I had nine months, maybe eight, to put the first book together. I did most of the work myself, putting in 12, 14 hours a day—it all felt a little crazy.

As the years moved on and the team grew, I just felt so lucky that I happened to be in the right place at the right time to be given the task of creating a publishing program. It was magic and such fun. I mean, I don't honestly think I could call it work. The team got on incredibly well; the office was full of laughter; and it was creatively very exciting. In all my career, I don't think I've ever been given that kind of gift—the opportunity to create a product with such potential and to grow a brand and build a strong list.

Giving up was very hard—the whole team felt like it owned the product. If you've worked for 12 years starting from nothing and created a range of books, it's difficult to hand the business over—it felt personal. But after so many years, I just trusted that a new team would take the product on and develop it further.   —Anne Marshall

Above, **THE UK** team created *Ripley's Kids Fun Facts and Silly Stories.*

Right, **THE TEAM** at the launch of book 8, *Strikingly True,* with Lizardman at the London Museum.

After a decade of producing Ripley books with its UK-based team, the operation was moved to Ripley Entertainment headquarters in Orlando, Florida, following Anne Marshall's retirement.

Left, INTERIOR SPREAD from Ripley's 2018, *A Century of Strange!*

Above, STARTING IN 2016, the US team launched board books for kids learning letters, numbers, shapes, and colors—illustrated by Ripley artist, John Graziano.

Above, THIS KING-SIZED Fun Facts & Silly Stories series features interactive puzzles, colorful pages, and fun lists plus unbelievable stories and photos.

Above, THIS UNIQUE trivia book compares events, inventions, and people that you would never believe existed at the same time in history.

Ripley Publishing's first foray into illustrated storybooks, *Bremner and the Party* and *Sharkee and the Teddy Bear*, both named after Ripley Aquarium mascots, were released in 2018. Entertaining "tails," the titles were written by Managing Editor Carrie Bolin, Editor Jessica Firpi, and drawn and hand-painted in watercolor by Ripley artist John Graziano.

Right, **PROMO** video featuring young Ripley fans retelling Sharkee and Bremner's stories in their own words.

Above, **AMANDA JOINER** illustrated by John Graziano

Anne and her team left some Robert Wadlow–sized shoes to fill, and it was my goal to carry on her legacy while expanding our book program in new directions, reaching new audiences, and building the Ripley brand. Publishing has come home, where we can provide better continuity and planning of our creative materials.

It's an exciting time for us, and there is never a dull moment. Only at Ripley's can someone with an accounting background, like myself, give editorial approvals one day and guide the world's smallest man around New York City the next!

—Amanda Joiner, Senior Director of Publishing and Licensing

Left, **ODD IS ART** pop-up gallery opening in Orlando, Florida, in May 2018.

Below, **DRAWING** inspiration from the eclectic, one-of-a-kind Ripley's archives and exhibits, the US team produced *Odd Is Art* in 2018. The title also featured artists that contributed to the Ripley collection by creating completely new pieces for display in the Odditoriums.

Digital Get Down

With such a vibrant history in print, radio, and TV, Ripley's has joined the digital age, engaging with people through every online avenue.

In an era when anyone can easily look up something they don't understand, Ripley's Believe It or Not! remains the authority on BIONs, ready to help introduce and explain the weird wide world. Content articles, videos, and even the cartoon have all made the Internet migration.

ripleys.com

An online presence has allowed the company to mobilize legions of enthusiastic fans from around the world who still submit their own BION stories, continuing the tradition of Robert Ripley. It even lets people see rare exhibits, sometimes even closer than they would at an Odditorium.

To date, Ripley's has published more than 1,000 blogs and amassed millions of online followers.

UNBOXING

YOUR FRUITS AND VEGGIES LIE TO YOU
COOL STUFF STRANGE THINGS

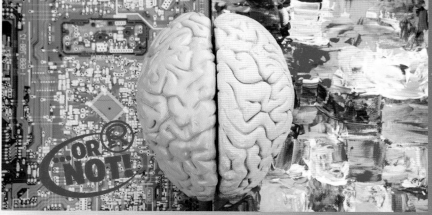
...OR NOT!
...OR NOT!

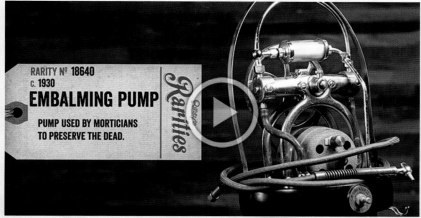
RARITY №18640
c. 1930
EMBALMING PUMP
PUMP USED BY MORTICIANS TO PRESERVE THE DEAD.
RIPLEY'S RARITIES

RIPLEY'S SIDESHOW

BOSTON TYPEWRITER CHESTRA
BION BRIEFS

the **MAN**

the **COLLECTION**

the **TRAVELS**

the **CARTOONS**

the **MEDIA**

▶ the **LOCATIONS**

the **COMPANY**

The Locations

Foreword by Bob Masterson

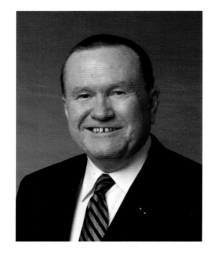

"I miss the brand itself. I miss its uniqueness and quirky nature. It's the heart of the company."

—Bob Masterson, previous President of Ripley Entertainment

Bottom, MASTERSON posing with the team at the San Francisco magic shop circa the 1970s.

BOB MASTERSON

I got my start with Ripley's shortly after my wife and I moved back to San Francisco in the mid-1970s. I was the guard at the front door of the *San Francisco Chronicle* newspaper. I didn't like it, so I was looking for a new job.

It wasn't long before I got a call wanting to know if I was interested in running a museum. I said, "Sure!" I had visions of fine art and statues and things like that—nothing like what I was about to encounter.

At the Ripley's Believe It or Not! museum, Chuck Thielen gave me the job as manager. This new job was part of a management training program set up by Alec Rigby, who owned Ripley's at the time. Alec was opening up new locations around the country and needed managers to run them.

I worked for Chuck for a year in San Francisco and then was transferred to the museum in St. Augustine, Florida—the oldest and most successful of the Ripley's attractions at the time and where Ripley intended himself to actually move to and have his attraction. I was the assistant manager there until January 1976.

It was in the midst of the only snowstorm to hit St. Augustine in 22 years that I drove up with my family to Gatlinburg, Tennessee, and took over as manager of the World of the Unexplained Museum. We had a magic shop and a big arcade, and even though it was successful monetarily, it was just the wrong location.

After a year, I took over the business in Myrtle Beach, South Carolina, which included not only a magic shop and arcade but also a bingo parlor. We had a parrot named Bingo that we would offer to give away, but it was so expensive no one could ever win it!

I was also in charge of Gatlinburg again—I had two shows there, as well as all the arcades, and we were building Ocean City, Maryland. Alec put me in charge of that, too, helping with the construction and organizing the staff. Eventually I ended up running the Magic Shops again.

In August of 1980, I was offered the job as vice president of operations in Toronto, and I came up and spent about 14 months there while my wife and kids still lived in Myrtle Beach. Eventually, we emigrated to Canada and became dual citizens.

In January 1985, Alec Rigby and John Withers sold the company to Jimmy Pattison, who owns one of Canada's largest companies, The Jim Pattison Group. Jimmy told me in one of our first meetings, "I want you to take $5 million and fix the attractions." This was right after John Withers and Alec Rigby told me I couldn't have $5,000 (unbeknownst to me, they were selling the company). So, he gave me $5 million and sent me out to fix up the attractions, which I did.

I became president of the company in November 1989. At the time, we had just 12 attractions: 8 Ripley's museums, 2 Museums of Witchcraft and Magic, Copenhagen Wax Museum, and Niagara Falls Wax Museum. I decided to focus on what we did really well, which was selling blocks of time to people to do something that's in the entertainment field. With that in mind, I knew that we could do more than just Ripley's Believe It or Not! museums. And once we agreed to that as a corporation, it opened up a whole new world for us.

The Locations

"I never doubted our ability to develop and run any business we decided to get into. I trusted our team."

—Bob Masterson

We started looking farther afield and built our first aquarium. We opened the Myrtle Beach Aquarium on June 13, 1997—Friday the 13th. It's been in business for more than 20 years. I think the Aquarium did more to change the company than anything. Throughout all the changes, Jimmy backed me 100 percent, and I will say that Jimmy Pattison Sr. is probably the one most responsible for my overall success.

People recognize the one-of-a-kind exhibits showcased in each Ripley's museum, but something else that makes this company unique are the buildings where the exhibits are housed.

I asked myself, how do you make the building itself an attraction? You see the answer in the façades of our museums. No two are alike. Each one is designed for the location and land it sits on, and I would say that adding unique buildings to Ripley's and to the attraction field in general is something I'll take credit for.

There is a time capsule—sealed in an air-tight, water-tight canister—buried under all the buildings we built. Each has certain things of importance as well as things that are just quirky. I'm very superstitious, and time capsules are part of that superstition.

There was a time when I knew pretty much everybody in the company—and we had well over a thousand people on staff. The first hour of every day that I came in the office I walked to each cubicle, every office, out in the warehouse and art department, to say hello to everybody. I loved the people.

I was with Ripley's for more than 35 years, and for more than half that time, I served as president of this great company. I met the people I respect the most in life, and I made my best friends during those years. My time as president was a dream come true for this guy from the south side of Chicago.

By the time I left the company in 2009, we had 94 businesses (some housed in the same facility) and franchise locations all over the world. Now Ripley's is known for more than just the oddities we collected—it's known for the odd, fun, and unbelievable buildings that house our great businesses and attract millions of visitors each year.

A good friend of mine is fond of saying "people get on the train, people get off the train, but the train keeps going." The Ripley Express has a long way to go before it reaches its destination, and the most exciting stops are ahead.

Left, **MASTERSON** with performer Erik Sprague, a.k.a. the Lizardman, at the grand opening of the Times Square Odditorium.

Top, **THE MARQUEE** display outside of Masterson's retirement event.

Bottom left, **CARTOON PANEL** drawn by John Graziano showcasing a "believe it or not" featuring Masterson.

Bottom right, **MASTERSON** receiving an award named in his honor from current Ripley president Jim Pattison Jr. at his retirement event.

1933 Chicago Odditorium

The first Odditorium was a temporary show at the Century of Progress World's Fair, but with its success, Ripley laid the foundation for today's 30 Ripley's Believe It or Not! museums in 10 countries.

As Ripley traveled the world, he continued to search for people with unusual features and abilities. He invited them to entertain at his parties, hired them to perform at his Odditoriums, filmed them, introduced them on his radio show, and of course, featured them in his famous *Believe It or Not!* cartoons.

The Chicago show, which closed and then opened again in 1934, featured a wide assortment of the strangest live performers ever gathered under one roof: characters like Alfred Langevin, who could blow up balloons with his eyes, and Joe Laurello, a.k.a. "the Human Owl," who could twist his head 180 degrees!

Above, **IT WAS** an illuminating experience for Russian Alvarez Kanichka—he swallowed live lightbulbs and then retrieved them by pulling on the electrical cord, still attached!

Above and right, **ALFRED LANGEVIN** of Detroit, Michigan, could blow up balloons, smoke a cigarette, and play a recorder—through his eye! He appeared at Ripley's Odditoriums from 1933 to 1940 and was featured in a cartoon as well as in a souvenir postcard for the 1940 New York City World's Fair Odditorium.

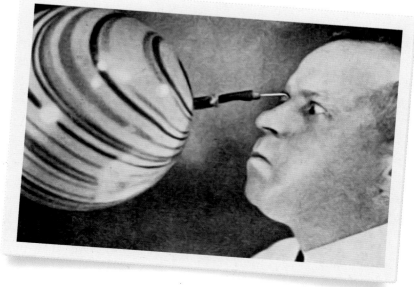

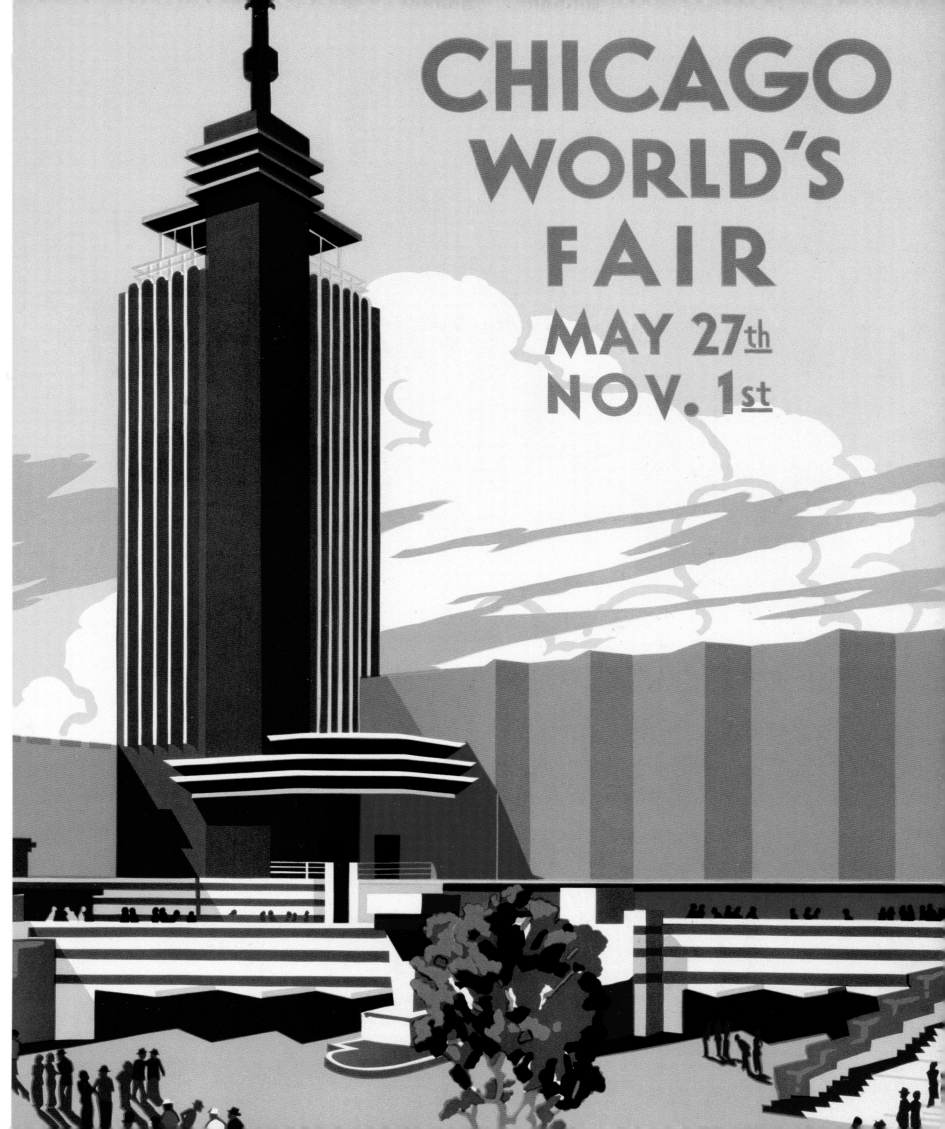

New York Odditorium

The Odditorium sensation swept the nation with popular appearances at world's fairs and expositions in San Diego, Dallas, Cleveland, and San Francisco, while traveling shows popped up in other cities. The permanent NY Odditorium located on 1539 Broadway, New York City, opened in 1957.

This page, **THE TEMPORARY** New York Odditorium located on 48th and Broadway debuted in 1939 and was only open for a year.

Believe *It or Not!*
Four Big Shows — One Admission
ROBERT RIPLEY'S $2,000,000
AIR-COOLED EXHIBIT OF
STRANGE OBJECTS and PEOPLE

THE **ODDITORIUM**
IN THE HEART OF NEW YORK CITY
AT 48th STREET AND BROADWAY

OMI the Tattooed Man (real name: Horace Ridler) appeared in the New York Odditorium in 1940. He was covered in tattoos from the top of his head to the soles of his feet. It took 15 million needle stabs to do the job.

Believe It or Not!
ODDITORIUM
Times Square - Broadway bet. 45th & 46th Sts., New York
PASS (1) ONE
GOOD WEEK DAYS ONLY
Valid Until_____
PRESS
Account_____
Issued by

OMI-OH, MY!
STRANGEST LOOKING MAN IN THE WORLD

Believe It or Not!
by Ripley

JUDGE DESMUKE ARMLESS KNIFE THROWER

THROWS 10 BUTCHER KNIVES WITHIN ONE INCH OF HIS WIFE STANDING 7 FEET AWAY

NOW APPEARING IN THE ODDITORIUM

IN 1939, Dagmar Rothman performed at the New York City museum, astounding crowds by swallowing and regurgitating a live mouse. He smoked a cigarette before and during the stunt, claiming that the smoke stunned the creature into lying still.

Above, JUDGE DESMUKE, the armless knife thrower, managed to throw 10 butcher knives that landed within 1-inch of his wife, standing 7 feet away.

The company got out of the live performance business shortly after Robert Ripley's death in 1949. Most states outlawed "freak shows" in 1972, and the custom has slowly died out since then. Shows like those at Ripley's Odditoriums in the 1930s and 1940s are a bygone phenomenon.

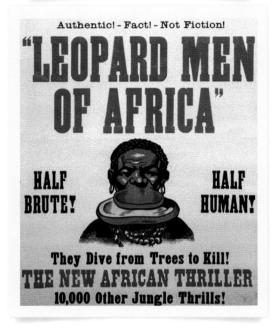

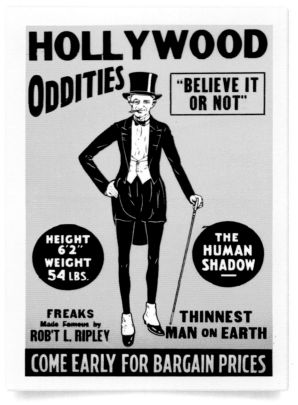

St. Augustine

Ripley's first, oldest, and largest permanent museum, St. Augustine was opened on December 9, 1950.

It is situated in a historic 1887 building, Castle Warden, that was a hotel once owned by Marjorie Kinnan Rawlings (author of *The Yearling*) and where Ripley himself stayed several times in the 1940s. Today, the 20,000-square-foot attraction boasts three floors of exhibits, including some of Robert Ripley's original collection.

IN 2004, Ripley's acquired the St. Augustine Sightseeing Trains, the iconic Red Train Tours.

ST. AUGUSTINE Museum façade in the 1950s.

A CROWD of guests walking through exhibits on display in the St. Augustine Museum in the 1950s.

TWO GUESTS looking at Robert Ripley's desk on display in the St. Augustine Museum in the 1950s.

Ripley's The Experience Begins At **Ripley's** GHOST TRAIN Adventure

OVER the years, the Ghost Adventure joined the St. Augustine family of attractions as well.

ST. AUGUSTINE'S **Ripley's** Believe It or Not! MUSEUM

Ripley's — Believe It or Not!

Niagara Falls

In 1963, Canadian entrepreneur Alec Rigby became a partner in the company and built the third Ripley's Believe It or Not! Odditorium. Located in Niagara Falls, Ontario, Canada, it is still in operation today.

1963

The Ripley's Believe It or Not! Odditorium in Niagara Falls has gone through a few changes since its opening in the '60s. There are now four attractions located in Niagara Falls:

- Ripley's Believe It or Not! Odditorium
- Guinness World Records Museum
- Louis Tussaud's Waxworks
- Ripley's Moving Theater

1985

PRESENT DAY

COME SEE
THE SHOW

RIPLEY's
Believe It or Not!

Times Square

After closing in 1972, the New York Odditorium returned to the big city in 2007, with the franchised location now on 42nd Street, between 7th and 8th Avenues.

RIPLEY'S Believe It or Not

PROUDLY FREAKING OUT FAMILIES FOR 90 YEARS

ODDITORIUM

Believe It or Not!

RIPLEY'S Believe It or Not!

THE RIPLEY'S museum façade at 45th and Broadway in New York City in the 1960s.

RIPLEY'S Believe It or Not! MUSEUM

RIPLEY'S Believe It or Not! MUSEUM

Cameras RADIOS GIFTS FILMS

THE BROADWAY BOOK SHOPS BOOKS GIFTS — SOUVENIRS TO-DAYS BEST SELLER

GAIETY MU AUDIO FIDE THE HIGHEST STANDARD IN

This page, **THE RIPLEY'S** museum façade at Times Square in New York City.

San Francisco

Under Alec Rigby, a permanent San Francisco Odditorium opened in 1966 on Fisherman's Wharf, a popular neighborhood and tourist area.

THE PRESENT DAY location also boasts Mirror Maze and LaseRace attractions.

ADVERTISING on a San Francisco cable car for the Ripley's Believe It or Not! Museum on Fisherman's Wharf.

This page, **THE RIPLEY'S** museum façade at the San Francisco World's Fair 1939.

Today, the company has 30 Ripley's Believe It or Not! Odditoriums operating in 10 different countries.

Continually adding new themed galleries, captivating video stories, interactive displays, and new artifacts to the collection—not to mention exterior and interior updates—has kept each location innovative and fresh over the years.

Amsterdam, Netherlands

Atlantic City, New Jersey

Baltimore, Maryland

Blackpool, England

Branson, Missouri

Cavendish, P.E.I., Canada

Copenhagen, Denmark

Gatlinburg, Tennessee

Genting Highlands, Malaysia

Grand Prairie, Texas

Guadalajara, Mexico

Hollywood, California

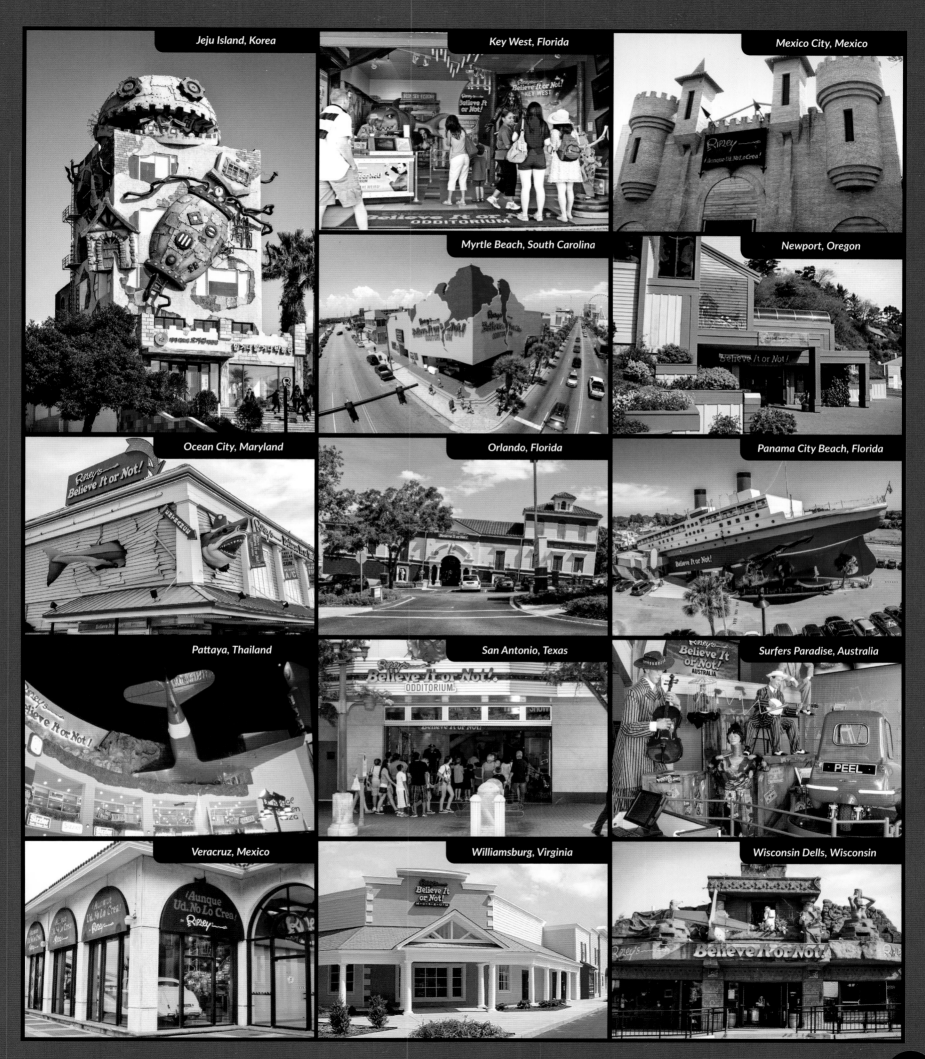

Jeju Island, Korea

Key West, Florida

Mexico City, Mexico

Myrtle Beach, South Carolina

Newport, Oregon

Ocean City, Maryland

Orlando, Florida

Panama City Beach, Florida

Pattaya, Thailand

San Antonio, Texas

Surfers Paradise, Australia

Veracruz, Mexico

Williamsburg, Virginia

Wisconsin Dells, Wisconsin

Present
Odditoriums

Vampire Killing Kit-c. 1850

Stories involving people rising from the dead, drinking blood, and changing into bats have persisted in Europe for hundreds of years. Known as "vampires", these ghoulish creatures can only be warded off or killed in a small number of ways according to legend. Travelers to Europe in the 19th century often carried a vampire killing kit like this set, which contains everything one would need to vanquish a vampire.

RIPLEY'S
Believe It or Not!
ODDITORIUM
ALL STRANGE! ALL TRUE!

Louis Tussaud's Waxworks

S ince the 1970s, Ripley Entertainment has been operating the world-famous Louis Tussaud's Waxworks attractions.

Locations:

- Grand Prairie, Texas
- Niagara Falls, Canada
- San Antonio, Texas
- Pattaya, Thailand

MOST of the wax figures are created by Ripley's in-house art department.

Guinness

In 1995, Ripley Entertainment secured a master license to operate and develop the Guinness World Records Museum attractions, and today there are five in operation.

Complete with trivia, memorabilia, themed galleries, and videos, the best part is that every guest can attempt genuine Guinness World Records titles live.

Locations:

- Copenhagen, Denmark
- Gatlinburg, Tennessee
- Hollywood, California
- Niagara Falls, Canada
- San Antonio, Texas

Aquarium of Myrtle Beach

In 1997, the company took its biggest step to diversifying its line of attractions with the opening of the first Ripley's Aquarium in Myrtle Beach, South Carolina.

Since its opening, more than 17 million visitors have toured the exhibits and galleries, including a 330-foot-long glidepath through an acrylic tunnel that lets guests view sharks, stingrays, sawfish, and a green sea turtle.

Left, **KEY STAFF**, including former president Bob Masterson (left), President Jim Pattison Jr. (second from the right), and former Gatlinburg attraction general manager Richard Weinberger (right) posing in front of a Myrtle Beach Aquarium billboard before its opening.

THE ACRYLIC TUNNEL has been an integral part of the Myrtle Beach Aquarium and a must-have for each Ripley's Aquarium thereafter.

INTERACTIVE experiences are available for guests of all ages.

I joined the company in June of 1998 and got to see Myrtle Beach for the first time about six months after the Aquarium opened. I was impressed. What struck me in particular was the design of the tunnel exhibit. Tunnel exhibits aren't very common in the United States to begin with, and those that exist are usually very short in length, so you don't get to appreciate the exhibit. Also, they're typically oddly shaped, which causes strange distortions. With Ripley's design, it was the opposite— it was circuitous, very lengthy, and not claustrophobic.

The pathway inside is over 8 feet wide, and a tall person could stand on his tippy toes, reach up, and still not touch the top of the acrylic. It has this beautiful uniform arc that—although it created a concave distortion, making everything look slightly smaller than it was—at least it was uniform so you didn't have sharks and fish weirdly going into a prism, disappearing, and then coming back out of the prism.

I saw the potential, and I thought, *If these guys can build an aquarium like this without having been in the aquarium business, just imagine what they could do if they had some help.*

—Joe Choromanski, former Vice President of Husbandry, Ripley's Aquariums

Aquarium of the Smokies

Guests can tour the Shark Lagoon through the 340-foot-long glidepath tunnel, as well as the popular Penguin Playhouse. Believe it or not, there are more fish in this Aquarium than there are people living in the entire town of Gatlinburg.

Finding a home in downtown Gatlinburg in 2000, Ripley's Aquarium of the Smokies has played host to more than 18 million visitors.

GUESTS can pet horseshoe crabs at the Discovery Center.

When we began designing Gatlinburg, besides the tunnels and the immersive theming, Bob Masterson wanted "big fish, colorful fish, lots of fish"—that was the mantra. He knew that people want it to be entertaining as well as educational. No one wants to come in and see an empty aquarium. They want to come in and be guaranteed to see a wild animal on every path through the tunnel. If you're going to have a sand tiger shark, you better have 12 of them so that everyone gets to see. No one wants an experience that's less than the person before them, and by following Bob's guidelines, we ensured that our guests will always have a great experience.

—Joe Choromanski, former Vice President of Husbandry, Ripley's Aquariums

Aquarium of Canada

After a little more than two years of construction, Ripley's Aquarium of Canada opened on October 13, 2013, resulting in an impressive downtown Toronto building.

Filled with flora and fauna found only in Canadian waters and classic, colorful species from the Indo-Pacific Ocean, the Aquarium exhibits its biodiversity at every turn. Visitors also get to explore a variety of immersive experiences, including a behind-the-scenes look at the complex life support systems.

YOUNG VISITORS can have fun with a trip down the iconic Nemo slide.

Below, **BOB KIRCHGESSNER** (left) oversaw the construction of all three Ripley's Aquariums. Steve File (right) specialized in the life support systems for each Ripley's Aquarium.

With Toronto, we designed it so you can navigate the whole Aquarium without an elevator or an escalator. The one thing we did different is on those ramps we put exhibits so that while people are walking down they can see more live exhibits. Going through the life support systems room is also a new experience. Wherever we could, we pushed the envelope to put more meaningful exhibitry. I think we hit a home run. I think Ripley's Aquariums are in the top tier because they hit what visitors really want to see.

—Joe Choromanski, former Vice President of Husbandry, Ripley's Aquariums

More Attractions

The Ripley's family has continued to grow, and now includes a plethora of family-friendly fun.

RIPLEY's
CANDY FACTORY™

RIPLEY's
MARVELOUS!
MIRROR MAZE™

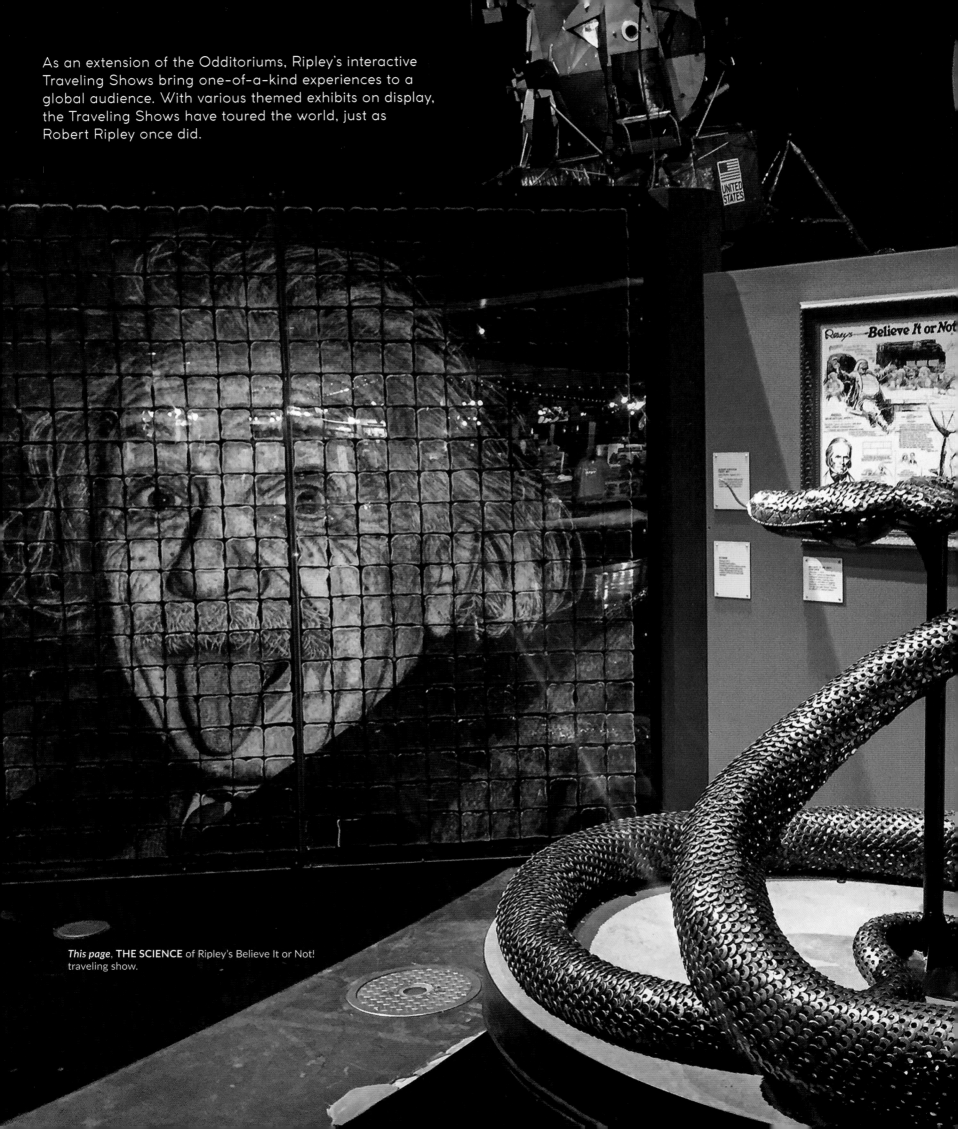

As an extension of the Odditoriums, Ripley's interactive Traveling Shows bring one-of-a-kind experiences to a global audience. With various themed exhibits on display, the Traveling Shows have toured the world, just as Robert Ripley once did.

This page, **THE SCIENCE** of Ripley's Believe It or Not! traveling show.

TRAVELING SHOW displaying artifacts from Japan, China, and India.

Believe It or Not!

Ripley's IMPOSSIBLE LaseRace

Ripley's SUPER FUN ZONE

the
MAN
the
COLLECTION
the
TRAVELS
the
CARTOONS
the
MEDIA
the
LOCATIONS
the
▶ # COMPANY

The Company

"You are only as good as the people around you, and we have some of the best, including our Ripley alumni!"

—Jim Pattison Jr., President of Ripley Entertainment

Foreword by Jim Pattison Jr.

One of the things that I truly love about Ripley's is the spirit of our founder Robert Ripley. He visited more than 200 countries in the 1920s, '30s, and '40s, when travel was much more complicated than it is today. A cartoonist but also a true adventurer, he brought back artifacts from all over the world to show everyone the real meaning of Believe It or Not!

It is this spirit of adventure and the passion for sharing amazing discoveries that underpins everything we stand for as a company today. We are a home for the unusual, the unbelievable, and the many global characters and diverse personalities that encompasses.

I joined Ripley's in 1990 from a sister company but in a completely unrelated field—banking, believe it or not! I was hired by company legend Bob Masterson and couldn't believe my good fortune during my orientation to visit so many cool locations where families were having fun together on their vacations. My first trips to familiarize myself with the company took me to Niagara Falls, Canada, the beach in South Carolina, America's oldest city of St. Augustine, Florida, and the mountains of Gatlinburg, Tennessee (gateway to the Great Smoky Mountain National Park), to name a few. I had always been fortunate to travel my whole life and being able to see our company's international destinations was also a special opportunity. We are in 10 countries today, so far, and there is lots to learn about entertaining our guests by respecting their cultures, religions, and economics while keeping it fun and educational.

What is fascinating to me is the company's growth over the last 34 years. Ripley's has always been opportunistic and, along with cartoons and book publishing, has been a consistent seller of attraction tickets around the world. Robert Ripley's original cartoon evolved into books, World's Fairs, live shows, Odditoriums and Wax Museums, Magic Shops, motion simulators, haunted houses, Guinness World Records attractions, world-class aquariums, traveling shows, and other fun family adventures.

The Ripley's world is filled with characters from performers featured in our books and cartoon, to our team members, who have very distinct and quirky personalities—even our accountants!

Truth is stranger than fiction, and we get the opportunity to tell those stories. We have been to Russia to buy submarines (we left empty-handed), visited Machu Picchu, the Great Pyramids in Egypt, the Great Wall of China, Easter Island, and many countries throughout the world. We've met the most interesting people, visited their homes, and seen their treasures. It is an amazing world.

After 100 years, the questions are always *What will happen next? How do we stay current?* The answer is by incorporating technology and adapting to the younger, always changing audience. Creating memories is a huge part of what we do, and it is so rewarding to see grandparents and parents bring the next generation to our attractions. We always strive to put a smile on their faces and create a memorable, photographable moment that will remain with them for the rest of their lives.

Our aquariums not only entertain but also educate visitors about the oceans and the need for conservation and treating our environment with great care. Being amazed by the unbelievable at our Believe It or Not! attractions, reading our books, or even setting a Guinness World Record at one of our venues—family fun is what we do and it is fantastic!

With more than 100 attractions around the world, we are busier than ever, and I can't wait to see what the next 100 years brings to our guests, fans, and team members.

I have been very fortunate to lead this company for a short period in its very long and fun history. However, you are only as good as the people around you, and we have some of the best, including our Ripley alumni! So many people have contributed to our success, but most importantly, we want to extend the biggest thank you to our millions of customers!

I can't believe I actually get paid for doing this!

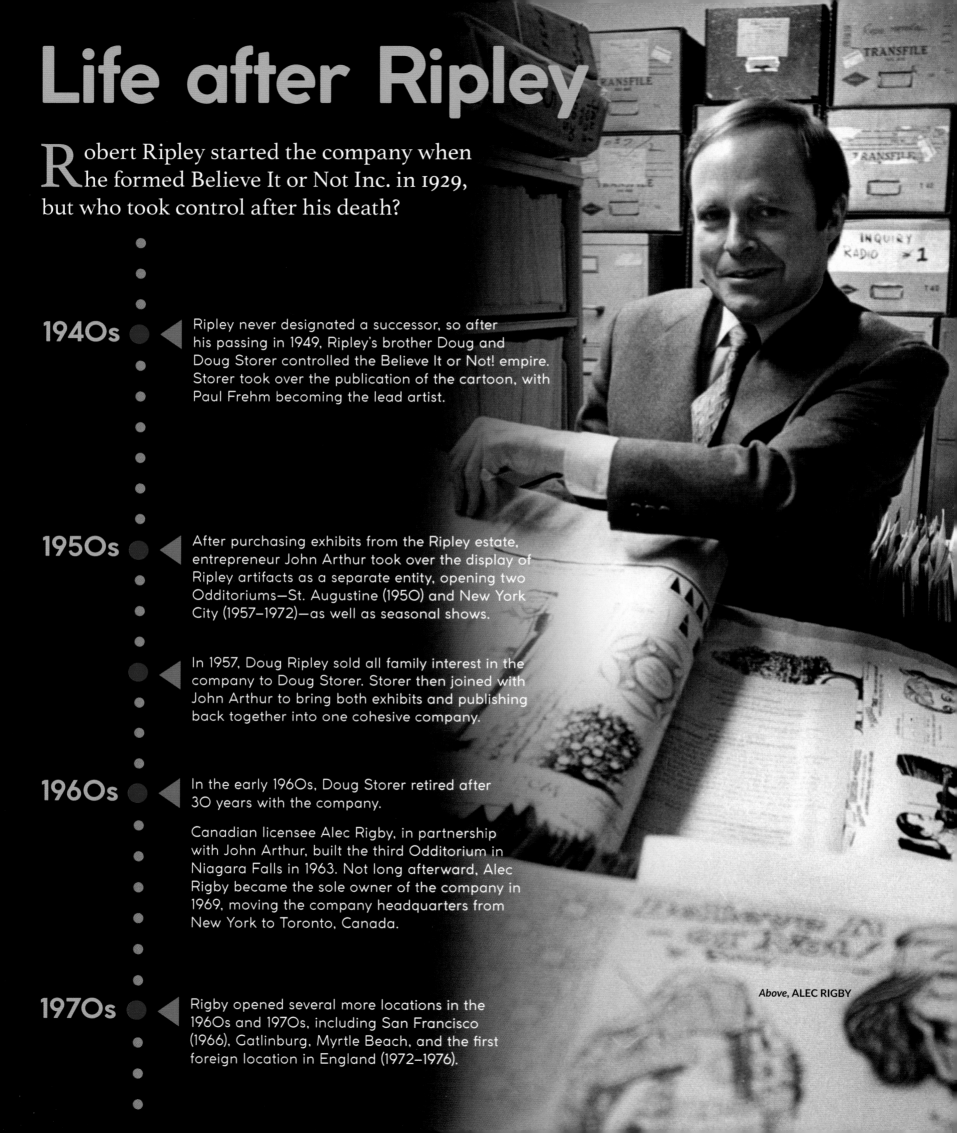

Life after Ripley

Robert Ripley started the company when he formed Believe It or Not Inc. in 1929, but who took control after his death?

1940s
Ripley never designated a successor, so after his passing in 1949, Ripley's brother Doug and Doug Storer controlled the Believe It or Not! empire. Storer took over the publication of the cartoon, with Paul Frehm becoming the lead artist.

1950s
After purchasing exhibits from the Ripley estate, entrepreneur John Arthur took over the display of Ripley artifacts as a separate entity, opening two Odditoriums—St. Augustine (1950) and New York City (1957–1972)—as well as seasonal shows.

In 1957, Doug Ripley sold all family interest in the company to Doug Storer. Storer then joined with John Arthur to bring both exhibits and publishing back together into one cohesive company.

1960s
In the early 1960s, Doug Storer retired after 30 years with the company.

Canadian licensee Alec Rigby, in partnership with John Arthur, built the third Odditorium in Niagara Falls in 1963. Not long afterward, Alec Rigby became the sole owner of the company in 1969, moving the company headquarters from New York to Toronto, Canada.

Above, ALEC RIGBY

1970s
Rigby opened several more locations in the 1960s and 1970s, including San Francisco (1966), Gatlinburg, Myrtle Beach, and the first foreign location in England (1972–1976).

With a background in theater set design, Derek Copperthwaite significantly improved the Ripley museum experience from 1962 to 1978 as the vice president of exhibits and design. After touring the New York City Odditorium in 1959, Copperthwaite contacted John Arthur with his ideas for how to enhance the appearance and inject some excitement into the displays.

He became an authority on the walkthrough type of attraction, helping Alec Rigby set up the Odditorium in Niagara Falls. Copperthwaite became heavily involved in research and development, as well as operations, training display personnel, installing new projects, managing all aspects of construction, and advising on marketing. He was integral to at least a dozen attractions, including Guinness and Louis Tussaud's.

JOHN ARTHUR (left) with Derek Copperthwaite

This page, **DEREK COPPERTHWAITE** working on setting up new museum displays in 1971.

1980s

The early 1980s saw Rigby—as sole owner and semi-retired company CEO—bring in John Withers to run the company as president. Under Withers, the company was able to license the successful TV show hosted by Jack Palance.

In January 1985, Ripley Entertainment (then known as Ripley International Ltd.) became part of the Jim Pattison Group (then Jim Pattison Industries) of Vancouver, British Columbia, Canada.

After John Withers retired from Ripley's, Bob Masterson became president in 1989, ushering in an era of growth as more franchised attractions opened all around the world.

1990s

In 1993, the company moved the headquarters from Toronto to Orlando, Florida, and started operating as Ripley Entertainment.

Ripley Entertainment diversified its line of attractions, which culminated in the opening of the Myrtle Beach Aquarium in 1997. Two more aquariums followed, with the Ripley's Aquarium of Canada in Toronto being the largest and most successful.

2010s

In 2010, Bob Masterson officially retired, and Jim Pattison Jr. became president, continuing the tradition of excellence in family entertainment.

Top, **ALEC RIGBY** at the opening of Blackpool, England, in 1972.

Second from the top, **JOHN WITHERS** with a mounted two-headed animal at his retirement event.

Above, **BOB MASTERSON** and long-time licensing agent Bob Whiteman.

Left, **NORM DESKA**, Bob Masterson, Edward Meyer, Mark Grunwald, and John Withers.

BOB MASTERSON, sitting on the left, with Jim Pattison Jr.

Unexplained Witchcraft & Magic

Every attraction has its day. During the 1960s and 1970s, the company owned and operated Witchcraft and Magic Museums, World of the Unexplained Museums, Magic Shops, and even bingo parlors.

HALLOWEEN wish-burning ceremony at the Museum of Witchcraft and Magic.

Halloween Wish-Burning

This page, **AT ONE TIME,** there were several magic shops around the country.

Bob Masterson explains how the Witchcraft and Magic Museum came to be:

Derek Copperthwaite had bought a great collection of witchcraft, historical items from the Isle of Man from Dr. Gardner in Castletown. Ripley's probably still has some of the books that were part of that collection. Some are very rare and old, handwritten in some cases, going back to the 1500s.

Derek bought this collection, and he built the Museum of Witchcraft and Magic in San Francisco, which was the perfect market for it.

A lot of the staff were Wiccans, and I remember one night finding a bunch of people in various stages of undress dancing around in one of the galleries looking at the sky in the middle of the museum. You just never knew what you'd find there!

—Bob Masterson

Above, **DRAWING** on the success of the San Francisco Museum of Witchcraft and Magic, a second location in Gatlinburg, Tennessee, was built. This in turn became the World of the Unexplained Museum, although it was mainly a witchcraft collection.

Cinema 180

During the 1980s and 1990s, Ripley's had Cinema 180 attractions, with three of them in the United Kingdom. The Cinema 180s consisted of short movies projected onto a giant, 180-degree domed screen. The idea was to create a feeling of total immersion for the viewer. The attractions moved locations and were later renamed Cinema USA.

Great Wolf Lodge

In 2006, the company opened its first venture into the hospitality industry, the Great Wolf Lodge Water Park Resort in Niagara Falls, Canada. At the time, this was the single largest Ripley attraction, encompassing 406 hotel suites and 94,000 square feet of indoor water park. The lodge was sold to another Pattison Group company in 2012.

Left, **JIM PATTISON** and Bob Masterson attend the grand opening of the Great Wolf Lodge in 2006.

I think one of the greatest things we did was the Great Wolf Lodge, which is not a part of Ripley's now. We bought the Canadian rights from one of the four partners who owned Great Wolf at the time. They had plans already done, but we had a great in-house architect who put it on steroids.

It is a spectacular top-rated resort in Canada—half-a-million people having a great time in one of the best indoor water park resorts. We built a great Aveda spa, created our own coffee brand—it is still so beautiful.

I would say Great Wolf Lodge was a big step for the company, like the Aquariums.

—Bob Masterson

Christmas Cards

Below, SANTA CLAUS, Indiana, cartoon from January 7, 1930.

BELIEVE IT OR NOT
(Copyright Registered U. S. Patent Office.)
— By Ripley

SANTA CLAUS
POST OFFICE
GENERAL STORE

THERE IS A SANTA CLAUS
SANTA CLAUS IS A LITTLE VILLAGE IN IND (50 people)
JAMES MARTIN - THE POSTMASTER, ACTS AS "Santa"
AND MAILED OUT
100,000
LETTERS 1929

Here Lies
the BODY of Wm SMITH
- of London
WHO CAME HERE
AND DIED
FOR HIS HEALTH
A GRAVESTONE ON THE ISLE OF WIGHT

THE PICTORIAL PINE
A CROSS SECTION OF THIS TREE
BORE THE LIKENESS OF A MAN
Donald Shaw
Buffalo

EARLY MAXWELL
OF the
(MEMPHIS SAUNDERS TIGERS)
MADE A BASKETBALL RECORD
OF 121 GOALS
IN SUCCESSION
(FREE THROWS)
Memphis
April, 1929

I n the 1930s, Santa Claus, Indiana, caught the attention of Robert Ripley, who then started a 90-year association with the town and a company culture surrounding Christmas that has outlasted the man himself.

Ripley featured the town in his syndicated *Believe It or Not* cartoon several times, which thrust Santa Claus, Indiana, into the national spotlight. The attention manifested in its little post office being flooded with more than a million pieces of mail.

The publicity generated by Ripley infuriated U.S. Postmaster General Walter Brown, and he threatened to force the town to change its name to ease the burden and avoid the Christmas season frenzy on the tiny post office—but not on Ripley's watch!

Ripley's wishes you Season's Greetings with the ancient gift of kings

Frankincense

Ripley's **Believe It or Not!***
Toronto, Ontario, Canada
Christmas 1989

Ripley's **Believe It or Not!**®

THE GREATEST GIFT

BELIEVE IT OR NOT!, DARIUS I, THE KING OF PERSIA IN 500 B.C. ANNUALLY RECEIVED 1,000 TALENTS —24.5 TONS— OF FRANKINCENSE FROM ARABIA WORTH $24,500,000 AT TODAY'S PRICES!

1989

"Silent Night"

DURING THE 1914 CHRISTMAS TRUCE OF WORLD WAR 1, SOLDIERS ON BOTH SIDES OF THE WESTERN FRONT SPONTANEOUSLY **STOPPED FIGHTING,** AND AGAINST THEIR COMMANDER'S ORDERS – CROSSED NO MAN'S LAND TO EXCHANGE GIFTS AND PLAY SOCCER!

2007

CHRISTMAS 2016
This Card is a Limited Edition

Ripley's **Believe It or Not!**®

MERRY CHRISTMAS
AND HAPPY NEW YEAR!
Ripley's - Believe It or Not -

SANTA CLAUS

AS THE PLUMP, JOLLY, RED-CHEEKED WHITE-WHISKERED INTERNATIONALLY RECOGNIZED ST. NICHOLAS, OF MYRNA, TURKEY, WAS CREATED BY CARTOONIST THOMAS NAST **OVER 150 YEARS AGO!**

45 4/500

JOHN GRAZIANO

2016

Ripley's **Believe It or Not!**

SANTA CLAUS

AS THE FAT, JOLLY, RED-CHEEKED WHITE-WHISKERED UNIVERSALLY RECOGNIZED ST. NICK WAS CREATED by Cartoonist *Thomas Nast* **100 YEARS AGO TODAY!**

In this spirit, let us wish YOU another 100 years of visits by St. Nick

RIPLEY Enterprises, Inc.
Empire State Bldg., New York I, N.Y.

1963

"LET IT GLOW!"

AMERICAN INVENTOR **THOMAS EDISON** (1847–1931) CREATED THE WORLD'S FIRST ELECTRICAL CHRISTMAS TREE LIGHTS IN 1882!

2013

HEY! ARE YOU THE GUY THAT SAID IN THEM "BELIEVE IT OR NOT" CARTOONS THAT THERE AINT NO SANTA CLAUS?

"BELIEVE IT OR NOT"

I WISH Eddie and his BROTHER "ST' ASTNY NOVY ROK RIP

Vintage Ads & Collectibles

Since the time of Robert Ripley, the company has been licensing the brand and its extensive content for advertisements and memorable products.

Above, **1932** Ripley's Disk-O-Knowledge, a spinning cardboard wheel that allowed the user to view BION stories in the die-cut cutouts, as well as on the back side.

Below, **1939-1949** Ink Blotters, paper used to absorb excess ink when writing with fountain pens.

Above, **1974** Milk Duds packaging.

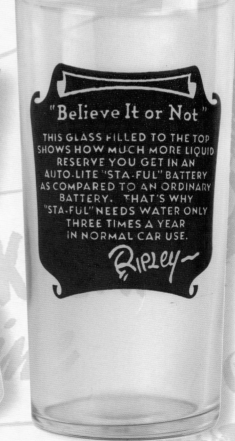

Above, Auto-Lite glass cup advertisement.

Above, Lotto tickets.

Above, 1975 Jim Beam cocktail napkins.

Above, 1982 Page Seed Company seed packages, featuring BIONs on record-setting produce.

Left, 1984 Hardee's Sports Oddities and Amazing Children.

Left, Jim Beam lamp.

Above, Themed calendars have been produced from the 1940s to present day.

Below, Playing cards, trading cards, and quiz game cards dating all the way back to 1934.

Below and right, Board games, computer games, and even a pinball machine.

Left and right, Fun products, like enamel pins, kids' science kits, invisible ink quiz books, antmobiles, and a bar apron.

Ripley's in Pop Culture

Have you seen them all? Whether it's a news segment on wild stunts, a blink-and-you'll-miss-it movie backdrop, or even a full-on mention, Ripley's has been appearing in media and pop culture for decades. These are just a selection from our cameo collection.

Above, **THE ANIMATED** movie *The Iron Giant* (1999) about a boy discovering a giant alien robot (voiced by Vin Diesel) has a blatant reference:

Hogarth: So we can't call Ripley's Believe It or Not, because. . . they wouldn't believe it.

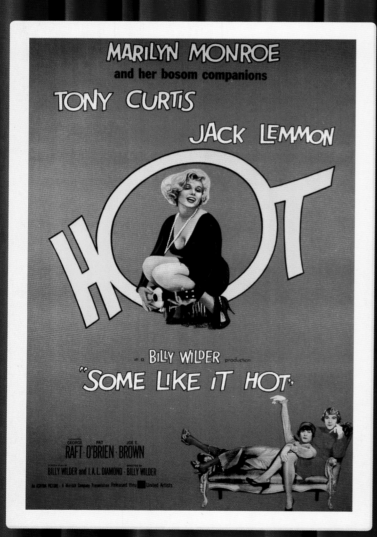

Above, **THE BLACK-AND-WHITE** film *Some Like It Hot* (1959) starring none other than Marilyn Monroe had a classic Ripley's mention:

Sugar: Believe it or not, Josephine predicted the whole thing.
Jerry: Yeah, this is one for Ripley.

Right, **IN SEASON 9** of Nickelodeon's *Spongebob Squarepants*, Sandy the squirrel tries to break every record in a parody book titled *The Guinness O'Ripley Enormous Book of Curiosities, Oddities, and World Records*. The episode, which aired in 2012, features records such as "longest tooth," "largest rubber band ball," and "most woodchucks chucked."

Left, IN Harry Potter (2010), Harry, Ron, and Hermione flee from Bill's wedding to Shaftesbury Avenue, the very corner where the London Museum stood.

Above, **THE MUPPETS** (2011) movie starring Jason Segel and Amy Adams has some choice lines:

"Oh, it was great. I went to Guinness Book of World Records. . . alone. Then Ripley's Believe It or Not. . . solo."

Left, **THE LONDON** race in *Fast & Furious 6* (2013) finds the "ride or die" crew hurtling through Piccadilly Circus and right by the old London Museum.

Pulitzer Prize-winning poet Kay Ryan (U.S. Poet Laureate 2008–2010) published *The Jam Jar Lifeboat & Other Novelties Exposed* with poems inspired by Ripley's Believe It or Not! She has stated, "For many years, I used 'Ripley's Believe It or Not' for an inspirational text. I had an old copy from the '30s.

It had the rough charcoal drawings that were just wonderful. I would open the book at random, when I wanted something to write about. . . I wrote scores of these Ripley poems. . . I'm attracted and repelled, and I think most people are. Ripley loved the grotesque and the extreme and the freakish and the weird and the tormented and the lost."

Below, **PAGES** from *The Jam Jar Lifeboat & Other Novelties Exposed,* with poems inspired by Ripley's Believe It or Not!

Poems by Kay Ryan

The Jam Jar Lifeboat
&
Other Novelties Exposed

Drawings by Carl Dern

WHOOPEE

The Mayor of Grand Lemps, France, issued an ordinance that any inhabitant may enter a saloon and drink his fill and then leave without paying. He was a prohibitionist.

Ripley's Believe It or Not!

This would take care of the bistros in short order.
There would be no point purveying liquor.
All the little drink saucers
that stacked on zinc counters
would go back to the cupboard.
The cheap heavy-based glasses
would be used for bud vases.
The prostitutes pimps lowlife scoundrels
and tired worn-faced working people
and mustachioed *patron* in an apron
and bright-buttoned *gendarmes* and
peasants with their crates of chickens
and baskets of produce from their farms
would all just have to go home.

In January 1986, cartoonist Jim Davis spoofed Ripley's Believe It or Not! with his panel *Garfield's Believe It, or DON'T!*

One 1939 *Looney Tunes* cartoon directly parodied Ripley's with the title "Believe It or Else" and featured a bucktoothed Egghead (later Elmer Fudd) wearing a suit and spats—Ripley's trademark look. An off-screen narrator begins the episode by saying in a voice eerily similar to Ripley's, "Ladies and gentlemen, Believe It or Else! I bring you right here tonight—odd and interesting facts that I have gathered from my many trips around the world."

As a teenager, cartoonist Charles Schulz submitted a drawing of his dog, Spike, and claimed he was "a hunting dog who eats pins, tacks and razor blades." Ripley featured the artwork and story in the February 22, 1937, panel. It was Schulz's first professional publication, and the sketch of the cute little dog would later become famous as "Snoopy" in the comic strip *Peanuts*.

Acknowledgments

COVER © Jo Hochmann, © pzAxe/Shutterstock.com; 7 (tl) Courtesy of Jim Pattison, (b) Courtesy of Jim Pattison Jr; 8 (bl) Courtesy of Jim Davis; 8–9 (bc) B. Gomer/Express/Getty Images; 9 (cl) Thomas S. England/The LIFE Images Collection/Getty Images; 12 (tl) Courtesy of Neal Thompson. Beowulf Sheehan Photography, (b) Courtesy of Neal Thompson; 13 (bl) Courtesy of Neal Thompson. K Pearlman Photography; 20–21 (bkg) © javarman/Shutterstock.com; 22–23 (bkg) © Victor Grow/Shutterstock.com; 34 (bl) Photography by Jessica Firpi; 55 (tr, cl) Ralph Morse/The LIFE Picture Collection/Getty Images; 56 (tr) Hulton Archive/Getty Images; 56–57 (bkg) © 895Studio/Shutterstock.com; 60 (bl) PA Images/Alamy Stock Photo; 63 (sp) PA Images/Alamy Stock Photo; 65 (tr) Cornell Capa/The LIFE Picture Collection/Getty Images; 71 (tr) Bettmann/Contributor via Getty Images; 74 (tr) Paul Fearn/Alamy Stock Photo; 75 (tr) GL Archive/Alamy Stock Photo; 85 (t) Public Domain {{PD-US}} NASA; 88 (t) Doug Schnurr/Alamy Stock Photo, (cl) Keystone-France/Gamma-Keystone via Getty Images; 96–97 © foxie/Shutterstock.com; 97 (bl) imageBROKER/Alamy Stock Photo, (br) Hypnox Photography, Wittypixel Photography, Isometric Studios, Matthew Russell Boman, Colin Gray, Cody Augustine, Ren Murray; 100 (bl) INTERFOTO/Alamy Stock Photo; 102 (bl) Mark Williamson Stock Photography/Alamy Stock Photo; 103 (tl) Lou-Foto/Alamy Stock Photo; 105 (tl) Oleksiy Maksymenko Photography/Alamy Stock Photo; 108 (cl) ZUMA Press, Inc./Alamy Stock Photo; 110 (bl) SONNY TUMBELAKA/AFP/Getty Images; 111 (br) John Lander/Alamy Stock Photo, Keute/ullstein bild via Getty Images; 112 (tl) Media Drum World/Alamy Stock Photo; 113 (sp) Konstantin Kalishko/Alamy Stock Photo; 114 (sp) ABIR ROY BARMAN/Alamy Stock Photo; 123 (b) Photography by Colton Kruse; 127 (sp) Bettmann/Contributor via Getty Images; 128 (b) Bettmann/Contributor via Getty Images; 128–129 © jannoon028/Shutterstock.com; 129 (bl) North Wind Picture Archives/Alamy Stock Photo; 140 (cl) © Arcady/Shutterstock.com, (b) © Jo Hochmann; 142 (tr) Bettmann/Contributor via Getty Images; 143 © Arcady/Shutterstock.com; 144 Courtesy of Don Wimmer; 145 (t) © Arcady/Shutterstock.com, (br) © Zadorozhnyi Viktor/Shutterstock.com; 146–147 (bkg) Photography by Rose Audette; 147 (br) Photography by Colton Kruse; 148 (l) © Jakub Krechowicz/Shutterstock.com; 149 (br) Photography by Jodi Thibodeau; 150 (tl) Photography by Jessica Firpi; 151 (br) Courtesy of James Proud; 159 (t) Courtesy of Warner Bros. Entertainment, Inc. All rights reserved; 172–173 © Tang Yan Song/Shutterstock.com; 176 (bl) Courtesy of Sony Pictures Television. All rights reserved; 176–177 (c) Courtesy of Sony Pictures Television. All rights reserved; 177 (tl, br) Courtesy of Sony Pictures Television. All rights reserved; 178–179 Courtesy of DHX Media. All rights reserved; 180 (tl, r, bl) Courtesy of Sony Pictures Television. All rights reserved; 181 (tc, cr, bl) Courtesy of Sony Pictures Television. All rights reserved; 182 (t) Courtesy of Sony Pictures Television. All rights reserved; 183 (tl, tr, cl, bl, br) Courtesy of Sony Pictures Television. All rights reserved; 191 (tc, tr, bl) Photography by Rose Audette, (br) Courtesy of Anne Marshall; 192 (tl) Photography by Rose Audette; 193 (c) Photography by Colton Kruse, (bl) Courtesy of Steve Parker; 194–195 (bkg) © mirtmirt/Shutterstock.com; 195 Photography by Colton Kruse; 203 (tl) John Phillips/The LIFE Picture Collection/Getty Images, (br) Public Domain {{PD-US}}; 216–217 Map created from https://www.maptive.com; 233 (tr) Courtesy of Guinness World Records; 235 (cr) Courtesy of Alice Edward, (tr, cl, bl, br) From Press Democrat, Santa Rosa, California, May 30, 1971, Medley Magazine; 243 (b) © MaxyM/Shutterstock.com, © Andrey_Kuzmin/Shutterstock.com; 250 (tr) The Advertising Archives/Alamy Stock Photo, (cl) Pictorial Press Ltd/Alamy Stock Photo, (br) © Nickelodeon/Alamy Stock Photo; 250–251 (bkg) © Markus Pfaff/Shutterstock.com; 251 (tr) © Tinseltown/Shutterstock.com, (tl) © Anton_Ivanov/Shutterstock.com, (cr) Photo 12/Alamy Stock Photo, (bl) Collection Christophel/Alamy Stock Photo, © Universal pictures international France; 252 (tl) GL Portrait/Alamy Stock Photo, (tr) Drawings © Carl Dern, Poems © Kay Ryan, (bl) © 1986 United Feature Syndicate, Inc. Drawn by Jim Davis, (br) Editorial/Alamy Stock Photo; 253 (tl) Moviestore collection Ltd/Alamy Stock Photo, (tr) Everett Collection, Inc./Alamy Stock Photo, (bl) © 1986 United Feature Syndicate, Inc. Drawn by Jim Davis; Master Graphics © Picsfive/Shutterstock.com

Key: t = top, b = bottom, c = center, l = left, r = right, sp = single page, bkg = background

All other photos are from Ripley Entertainment Inc. Every attempt has been made to acknowledge correctly and contact copyright holders and we apologize in advance for any unintentional errors or omissions, which will be corrected in future editions.

Connect with **Ripley's** — Online or in Person

Stop by our website daily for new stories, photos, contests, and more! **www.ripleys.com**
Don't forget to connect with us on social media for a daily dose of the weird and the wonderful.

 /RipleysBelieveItOrNot

 @Ripleys

 youtube.com/Ripleys

@RipleysBelieveItorNot

"*I believe Ripley's is just getting started.*"

—Jim Pattison

Ripley "BELIEVE IT OR NOT."